A SPECIAL VILLAGE IN LONDON

By Andrew Wilson

Sponsored by

To my lovely wife, Diana, my number one supporter.

Clockwise from top left: Wandsworth Bridge, All Saints Church, Parsons Green and The Hurlingham Club.

Contents

A Short History of the Area	6	Wandsworth Bridge Road	110
All Saints Church	10	Chelsea Football Club	112
Fulham's Bridge	**20**	Surrey Classic and Prudential 100 Cycle Race	116
Bishop's Park from the River	26	**Open Spaces**	**118**
Bishop's Park	32	Fulham Palace	120
Fulham Football Club	46	Fulham Palace Allotments	128
Farmers' Market	52	Hurlingham Park	130
Alphabet Streets	54	Polo at Hurlingham Park	138
Riverside Walk to the Crabtree Pub	58	The Hurlingham Club	142
Street Scenes	**66**	South Park	146
A stroll around Sands End	68	The Queen's Club	162
A walk around Fulham	74	Eel Brook Common	170
Fulham Broadway	82	Fulham Cemetery	176
Fulham Road	86	Normand Park	180
Munster Road	90	**The Riverside**	**182**
New King's Road	94	The Boat Race	188
North End Road	98	Fulham Railway and Footbridge	190
Parsons Green	102	Wandsworth Bridge	200
Parsons Green Fair	108		

NEW FEATURE
Local walks
New to the Wild About series are the local walks allowing you to really get to know the area as depicted in each book. *(See page 68 and 74)*

Welcome to Wild About Fulham

Welcome to the eleventh book in my ever expanding series of photographic books on the South West of London. I am not sure why it took me so long to do, I live just across the river in Putney and my Putney book came out three years ago. Anyway, as the saying goes, better late than never. Just like its near neighbour, Fulham has all the best ingredients; a wonderful bridge and river that we share, some truly wonderful open spaces (if you thought that the avenue of plane trees in Wandsworth Park were awesome then you are in for a treat once you step inside Bishop's Park, where dare I say the avenue is even more impressive). It has some iconic clubs from Queen's to The Hurlingham, two football clubs, plenty of places to shop from the Fulham Road to the New King's Road and simply oodles of history.

My books take over a year to produce and in that time I really feel I get to know an area. I love walking, just as well you might say, but one particular joy with this project was the walk from Putney Bridge, through Bishop's Park and along the river to The Crabtree pub and beyond. For those familiar with my work, I have expanded this theme with my latest book and worked with my local historian, Caroline MacMillan, who was born in Fulham, to bring you two expertly devised walks, which really brings alive the local area and all it has to offer. Fulham is steeped in history and it was great fun roaming the area and pulling together this latest collection of pictures.

As with all photographic assignments of this kind, it is never a one man show and there are numerous people to thank. Firstly, my historian and writer Caroline MacMillan. I met Caroline last year when we collaborated on my Hammersmith book and it was brilliant to discover that she was born in Fulham, which gave us the perfect excuse to work together again. My graphic designer, Tim Ball from Ball Design & Branding in Kingston, who has now worked with me on my last nine projects and is brilliant at bringing my photography to life. Frank Harrington from Atlantic Plumbing & Heating, a super local company who kindly agreed to help me with some sponsorship. The ladies from the local 'news' organisation, Those Who Nose Fulham, who passed on some great advice about what I might like to capture photographically. My new PR lady, Julia Laflin, who lives locally and has been a brilliant help. I would also like to thank the countless people who helped me gain access to certain places, where permission would be required and are mentioned within the text. For the second year I would also like to thank Roehampton University for again providing me with an excellent intern, Alexis Wilson (no relation), who has been invaluable whilst we have brought this book to print, together with two others. Finally, I would like to thank Allan and Cindy Fuller from Allan Fuller Estate Agents, who approached me to do this project. They love what I do and they kindly agreed to sponsor this book, which neatly ties-in with their brand new Fulham office. I love photography and being able to work on this over the past 18 months has been a pure joy and I hope a little of that passion leaps off the page as you review my latest collection of photographs.

Andrew and Josie

Left: Josie, my springer spaniel and constant companion, lying amongst the daisies in Pineapple Park.

Fulham

A SHORT HISTORY OF THE AREA
by Caroline MacMillan

Coins unearthed during excavations near Fulham Palace indicate a Roman presence during their four centuries of settlement from 43AD. After the Romans departure the Anglo-Saxons who landed their boats on the firm gravel near to where Putney Bridge stands today would have found the only inhabitants of the woodlands to be deer and wild boar. Until two hundred years ago Fulham remained virtually an island, the Thames forming its south and western boundaries, a tributary of that river its eastern edge and a stream dividing it from land to the north. Whilst the water courses to the east and north now run through underground culverts, the tidal river continues to flow along its remaining edges.

The first mention of the name of Fulanham, Fulla being an Anglo-Saxon name and Hamm meaning low lying land within the bend of a river, was when the manor was granted to Waldhere, the fifth Bishop of London in the early 8th century. The extensive manor lands included Hammersmith which was known as North Fulham until the two parishes were created in 1834. The Bishop of London ceased to be Lord of the Manor in 1868 whilst the moated Palace continued as their summer home until 1973.

By Tudor times Fulham was a sparsely populated agricultural area with wheat, fruit and vegetables benefitting from the rich soil of Fulham Fields and the river providing a livelihood for fishermen and watermen. The quiet country locality was favoured by the rich and Sir Nicholas Crispe, a supporter of King Charles I, built impressive Brandenburg House on the riverside borders of Fulham and Hammersmith. Today's roads of Munster, Peterborough, Colehill, Ranelagh and Hurlingham are all reminders of former estates with imposing houses.

By the seventeenth century dwelling houses sprawled along Fulham High Street, then known as Berestrete meaning 'near the burg or Manor House'. Law and order was maintained by a constable appointed by the Manor Court and miscreants locked in the caged watch-house. Boats landed nearby and an alehouse, The Bell, was established where The Eight Bells stands today. As well as small riverside hamlets at Crabtree and Broomhouse, communities were growing around Parsons Green and North End although the population overall remained very small partly due to periodic outbreaks of plague which at one time necessitated a pest house in Hurlingham Fields. The manor came under the control of Oliver Cromwell's government during the Civil War but Fulham suffered little material damage though some local men fought on one side or the other. After the Restoration John Dwight, who had been granted a patent by

Below: Fulham road at the Crookham Road junction today (left) and in 1904 (right). Thanks to the Hammersmith and Fulham archives for allowing reproduction of the black and white images (below left, opposite and overleaf).

Charles II to make 'China and Persian ware' or what we know as porcelain, built a kiln near the junction of Fulham High Street and New King's Road, and so began a long tradition of pottery manufacture in Fulham.

With the country's stability restored, the City of London continued to expand westwards. Farmland replaced Fulham's woods and the clay soil was dug to provide bricks, often creating lakes four feet deep. Nearer the river the good soil encouraged farmers to grow soft fruits such as strawberries and gooseberries whilst orchards produced apples and plums, all of which could be taken to Covent Garden by boat or carried in panniers made by osiers from riverside willows. Grand houses with even larger gardens required ready grown plants to decorate their grounds and by the early 18th century Fulham Nursery was established between Hurlingham Road and the New King's Road. With travellers bringing back new plants to this country for well over a hundred years Fulham became an important centre for horticulture with the Rench and Veitch families who owned extensive land near Broomhouse Road introducing many foreign species including Auriculas and the Chinese Strawberry whilst the Bagley family specialised in fruit and nut trees.

Apart from a temporary pontoon bridge built by Parliamentarians in 1642, the need to replace the ferry between Fulham and Putney increased but despite loud protestations from watermen for loss of business, a long wooden toll bridge was opened in 1729 with the Prince of Wales being the first person to cross in a coach. This structure lasted for over 150 years when it was replaced by Sir Joseph Bazalgette's classical design which could not be more different from his ornate Gothic bridge further upstream at Hammersmith.

Whilst some estates prospered, others were not so fortunate and Sandford Manor House near Sands End became a factory for saltpetre which was a constituent of gunpowder, then a pottery and finally housed a cloth making manufacturer. In 1824 the estate was purchased by the Imperial Gas Light & Coke Company who erected the first gas holder with three more in the following few years. As well as providing work for hundreds of local residents,

Above: A view from the Putney Wharf in 1962 and above it today. Thanks to Sarah Dorin for letting me take the photograph above from her apartment in Putney Wharf. What a view!

the gas works played an important role in the development of this part of Fulham and by the end of the century its many industries included the Sunlight Laundry, William de Morgan's pottery kiln, MacFarlane Lang's biscuit factory and Kop's Brewery who produced a non alcoholic beer. Busy wharves lined the river's edge at Sands End and also north of Fulham Town where the Haig and Booth families established a distillery and Manbre Saccharine Company built their factory.

By 1901 the population of the area had increased to more than 137,000 and the remaining estates were attracting developers.

Dorset builders Gibbs and Flew turned their attention to the North End and built roads of grander houses, renaming the area West Kensington which they hoped (unsuccessfully as it turned out) would tempt rich buyers from the real Kensington. Jimmy Nichols purchased much of the Peterborough Estate, its house by now a lunatic asylum, and by the end of the 19th century the wide streets were lined with his distinctive terraced houses, each adorned with a trademark terracotta lion.

The Elementary Education Act of 1870 resulted in the need for more schools. All Saints' School in Fulham High Street had been established in the seventeenth century and was now joined by many others including the magnificent Tudor-Gothic Elizabethan School, formerly a Ragged School, and Lady Margaret on Parsons Green. Fulham Workhouse in Fulham Palace Road became the local hospital and was eventually rebuilt to accommodate Charing Cross Hospital when it transferred from central London.

To accommodate the needs of the ever growing population All Saints church was rebuilt in 1881 to a design by Sir Arthur Blomfield, the architect son of a Bishop of London. Whilst parts of the original tower date back to the fourteenth century during the rebuilding work a stone attached to a window jamb was uncovered confirming that a place of worship had been at this riverside location since the twelfth century.

New parish churches were also consecrated including St. Dionis at Parsons Green in 1885 which was funded from the sale of the redundant Sir Christopher Wren church of St. Dionis Backchurch in the City whilst St. Andrew's in Greyhound Road has bells from another demolished Wren church which are reputed to be the oldest in London being the only ones to survive the Great Fire. The needs of the growing Catholic community were met in 1847 by the building of the church of St. Thomas of Canterbury in Rylston Road splendidly designed by Houses of Parliament architect Augustus Pugin. The Methodist Church of 1897 in Chesson Road has not stood the test of religion's time eventually becoming a bedding centre and is now being developed for residential purposes whilst the Congregational Church in Castleton Road off North End Road is the Bhavan Centre of Indian Culture and a reminder that Mahatma Ghandi lived nearby in Barons Court whilst studying to become a barrister.

Sitting in the loop of the Thames, Fulham escaped much railway development. The Metropolitan line was extended from Gloucester Road to West Brompton in 1871 and finally through to Wimbledon in 1889. This has resulted in wheeled vehicles being the main means of transport with inevitable traffic jams which today's travellers along Fulham Palace Road know so well.

Whilst North End Road Market is a constant reminder of the area's rural past the independent butchers, bakers, shoe makers and oilmen have long disappeared to be replaced by supermarkets and coffee chains and a shopping mall awaits those arriving at Fulham Broadway underground station. Gone too is the Grand Theatre near Putney Bridge and the Granville Music Hall at Jerdan Place where George Robey and Marie Lloyd played to full houses.

Despite its urban location Fulham has strong sporting associations and whilst tennis at Queen's Club and croquet at the Hurlingham Club is restricted to members only, the Boat Race is available to all and thousands line the river's bank each spring to cheer crews from Oxford and Cambridge Universities as they row from Putney to Mortlake. Fans regularly stream over the boundary from Chelsea to their football ground located on Fulham soil and home supporters cheer Fulham at their Craven Cottage riverside home.

Fulham may have been a virtual island years ago but it is now a vibrant part of the capital city and those who live there enjoy the open aspect of the ever changing tidal river and green open spaces which sit alongside the smart boutiques of the New King's Road and many restaurants – all just a stone's throw away from central London.

Caroline MacMillan, 2015

Below: The Town Hall on Fulham Road today (left) and mid 1910s (right).

Fulham

This map was kindly supplied by local artist, Kate Fishenden and is not meant to be absolutely to scale but to give the reader a fun introduction to the area and some of the places covered in this book. She can be contacted via her website *www.starchgreen.com*

All Saints Church

The original Victorian lamps which date back to 1886 were refurbished when Putney Bridge underwent major repairs in 2014.

Anyone for a taxi? We don't suggest you hail this particular cab as it's owned by our sponsor, Allan Fuller.

Left: All Saints Church Cemetery from the church's tower. In the early 19th century Fulham's secluded graveyard was targeted by body-snatchers and often relatives would take turns to guard the grave of a loved one at night. The last record of a snatch was in 1828.

Thank you to Lidija, Putney Bridge Premier Inn's manager, for allowing me to take this shot, and the one on page 24, of All Saints Church from the roof of the hotel.

Thank you to Edmund Hartley for guiding me up the church tower from where I took this photograph and the one on the previous page. The London Clipper Boat pictured runs a regular service between Putney and Blackfriars.

Right: The delightful gothic style Pryor's Bank Cafe viewed on a snowy morning. The Pavilion and surrounding garden were opened in 1900 to provide welcome light refreshments for visitors to Bishop's Park whilst newspapers and illustrated weekly and monthly magazines were available for customers in the designated reading room.

All Saints can look good whatever the season, whatever the angle, and particularly when the magnolia is in full bloom.

Fulham's Bridge

Until 1729 a ferry was the only means of travelling from Fulham to Putney. The right to operate the ferry belonged to the Bishop of London who in turn sublet to ferrymen who would pay the Bishop one farthing for each parishioner carried, one half-penny for non-parishioners whilst horses cost a little more. Those using the ferry often found it a hazardous journey as Archbishop Laud noted in his 1633 diary when his horses and men sank to the bottom of the river when the over laden ferry boat struck rough water. Fortunately all lives were saved, both animal and human.

Despite objections from ferry men that it would affect their livelihood and those who argued that a bridge would affect the tidal flow of the river, an Act of Parliament was passed and in 1729 Fulham Bridge, as it was known then, opened. A 768 ft long wooden construction with 26 narrow openings it was the only bridge between London Bridge and Kingston. Four toll men, each provided with coat, hat and staff were engaged on wages of ten shillings a week to manage the toll houses each end of the bridge.

The abolition of tolls in 1877 spelt the doom of the bridge and Sir Joseph Bazalgette was commissioned to design a new one. He selected a route just west of the old bridge on the line of the Chelsea Waterworks aqueduct and his classical design consisted of five arches made from granite from Aberdeen and the Prince of Wales's own quarries in Cornwall. Since opening in 1886 it has been widened twice to accommodate the ever increasing flow of traffic and has become the busiest Thames crossing upstream from Westminster.

Previous Page: Attempts to build a permanent crossing over the river were initially thwarted by strong opposition from the ferryman but a wooden bridge, known as Fulham Bridge, eventually opened in 1729. Until 1877 it was a toll bridge though the Bishop of London and his household were exempted from payment, a privilege often abused by those with the nerve to walk or drive across shouting 'Bishop'.

Pictures of Sir Joseph Bazalgette's elegant stone bridge that opened in 1886 on the line of an aqueduct which previously brought water from south of the river to homes on the northern side.

Bishop's Park from the River

Inset: Many thanks go to Sarah Dorin for the autumn shot of Bishop's Park from her apartment in Putney Wharf.

A close encounter with swans on the Thames with Bishop's Park in the background

Josie enjoying a paddle on the foreshore in Putney

Bishop's Park

The Bishop of London's gift of Bishop's Meadow for use as a public park was not quite as generous as first appeared. Lying between the Fulham Palace moat and river over the years, it had become very marshy, was prone to flooding from the polluted river and had been used as a rubbish tip.

To prevent flooding an embankment wall was built in 1893, the cost of £12,000 being met by Joseph Mears, a local resident and founder of Chelsea Football Club.

The riverside walk is equally beautiful throughout the seasons.

The avenue of lofty plane trees in autumn (right), winter (bottom left) and spring (top left) are a major feature in the park and were planted in 1893.

Overleaf: A junior football session being coached on the open sports field in Bishop's Park.

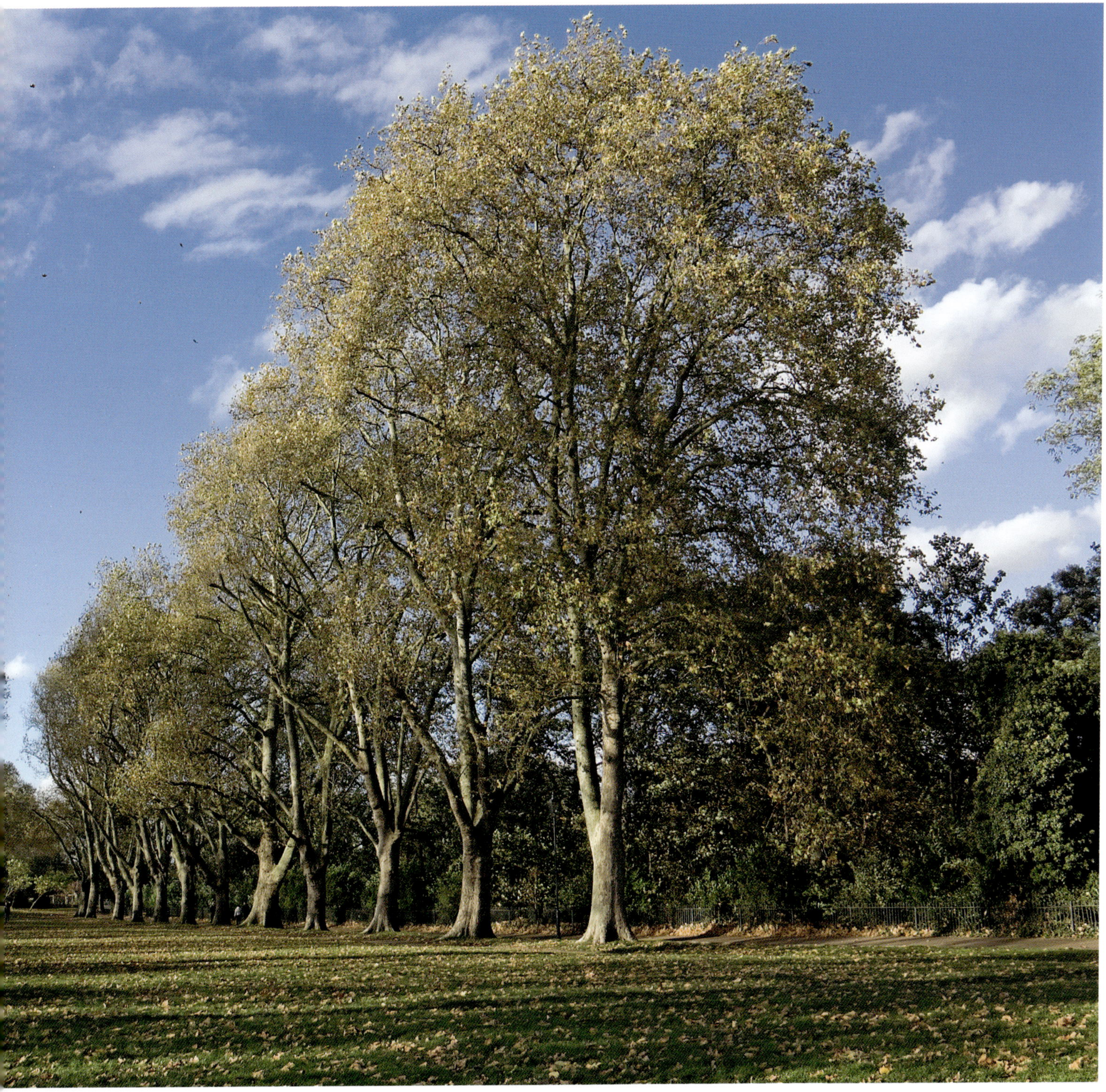

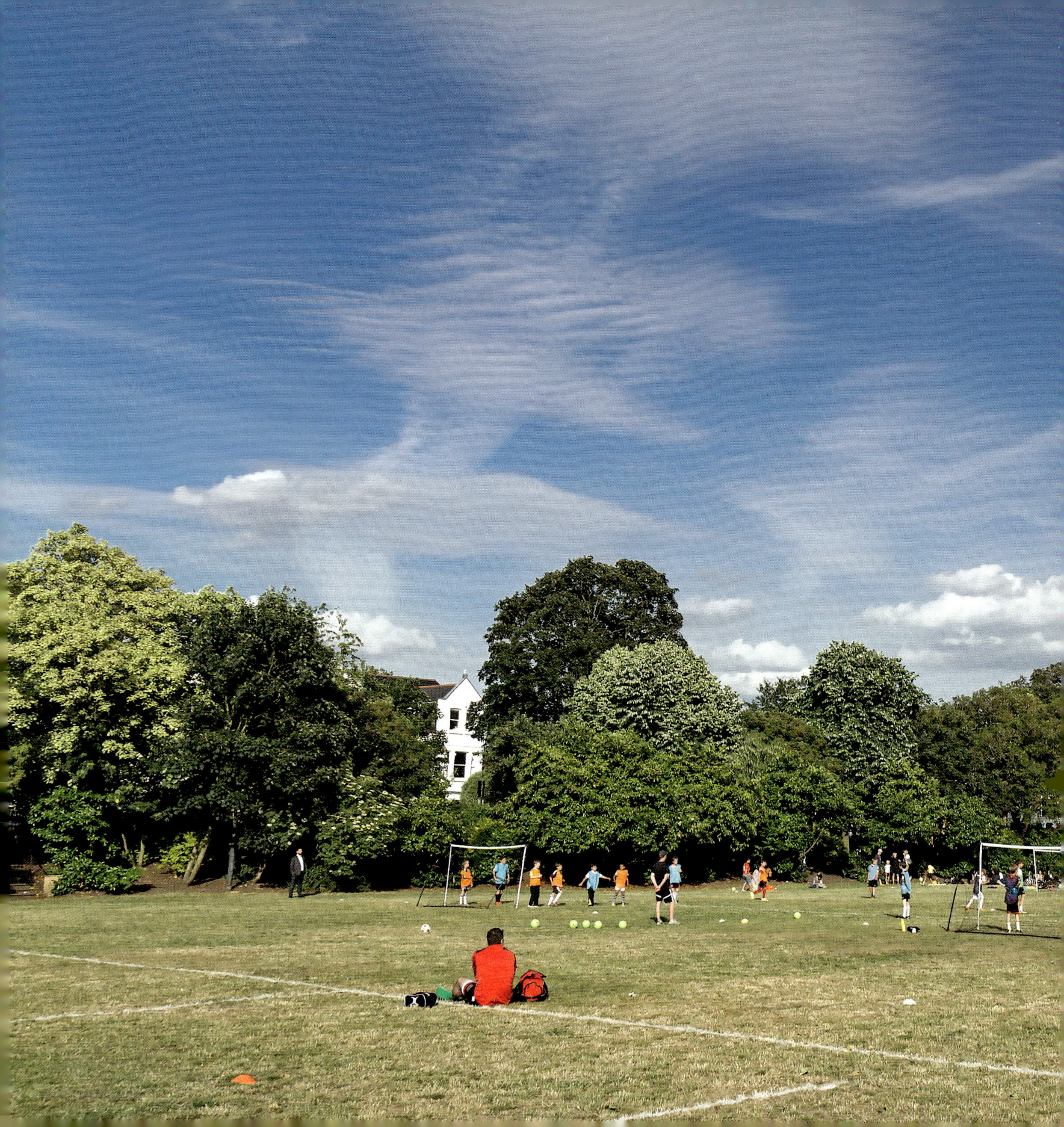

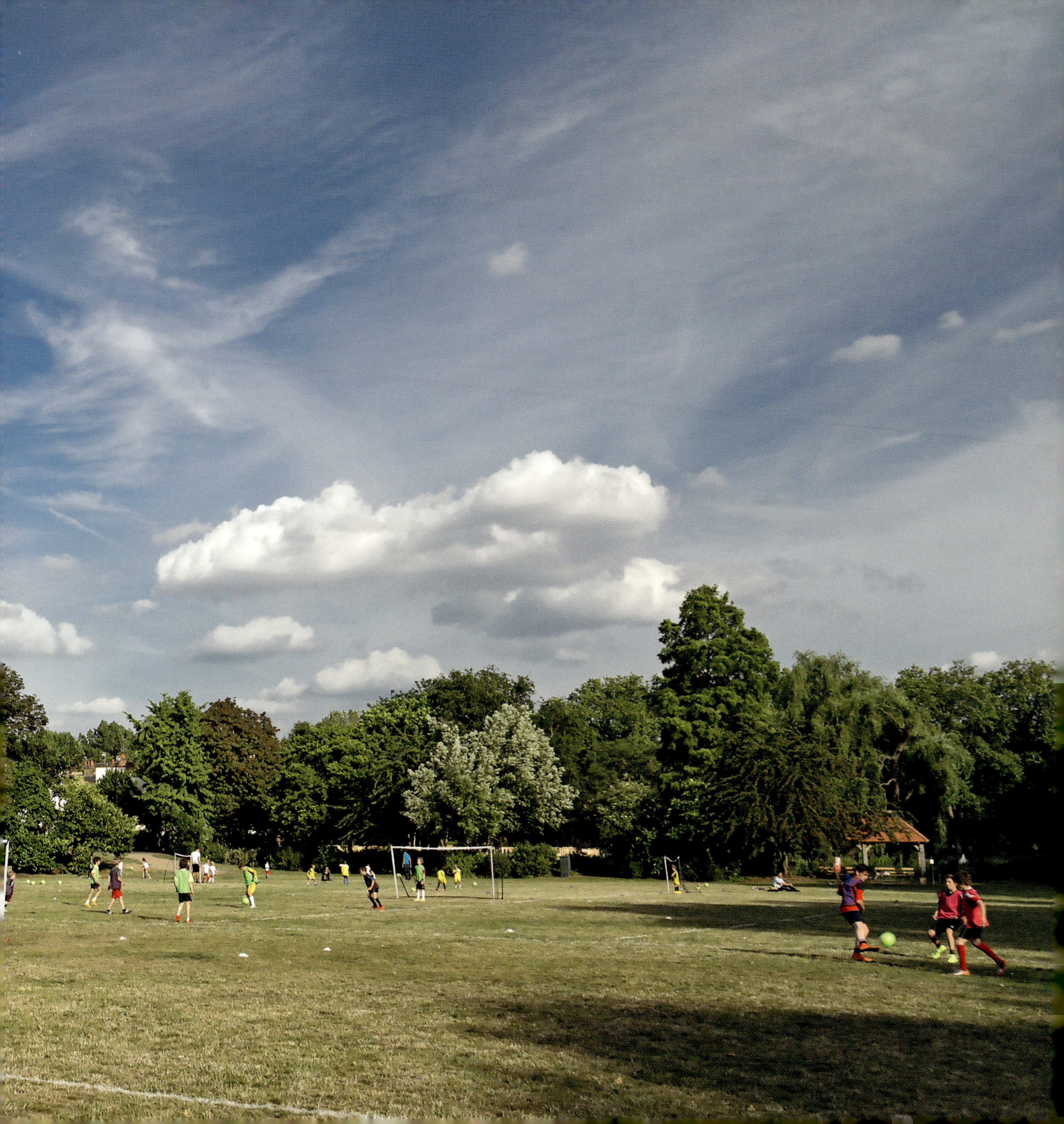

40

The M525 is a popular mode of transport to the youngest visitors to the play area.

Opposite: The skate park was opened in 2012 and has since played host to several skate competitions.

41

Left: Bishop's Garden Cafe is an ideal stop after a stroll in the park.

Opposite: To Josie's dismay, dogs are not allowed in the park's lake area.

43

The ornamental lake and paddling area were restored to their former glory in 2012.

Fondly known as 'Margate Sands', after a recent face-lift the urban beach is proving a popular attraction on sunny days.

Fulham Football Club

The statue of Johnny Haynes, considered to be Fulham's best player. He was a capped for England 56 times, 22 of those as captain and played a record of 657 games for his club where he was fondly known as 'The Maestro'.

Fulham Football Club, founded in 1879 by lads attending nearby St. Andrew's Sunday School, moved to their new home in 1896 when they acquired the derelict thatched Craven Cottage which had been badly damaged by fire. The original 18th century cottage was built by Baron Craven and stood where the centre circle is marked on today's pitch.

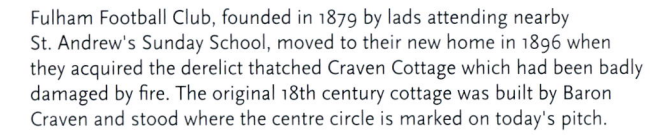

Top left: Football crowds streaming down the tree lined walk between the Palace grounds and river embankment and are virtually walking on water as they follow the course of the now filled in moat.

On the day that the photographs were taken outside the ground it was the last home game of the 2014/15 season. It turned out to be an amazing game with Middlesbrough needing a win and ending up losing 4–3.

49

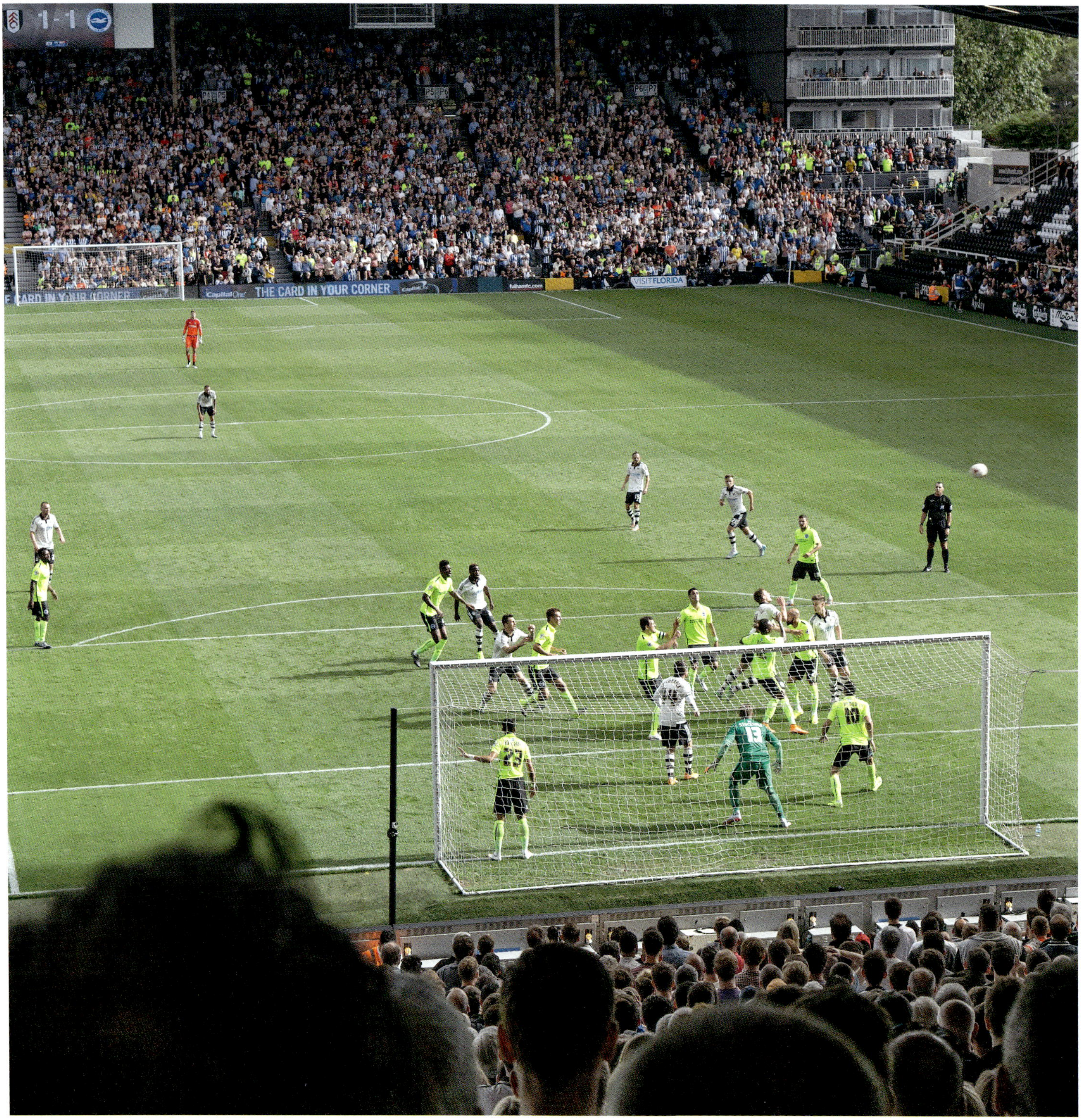
1-1
THE CARD IN YOUR CORNER
VISITFLORIDA

Opposite page: The pictures on these two pages and the Riverside Dogs picture (on the previous page) were all taken at the home game against Brighton this season (2015/16).

Top left: I met several friends at the game; Julian, a fellow photographer, has been an ardent fan since he was a small boy.

Bottom left: The mascot of the team fools around at the side of the pitch.

Bottom right: Fans stream across Putney Bridge.

Many thanks to my good friend and season ticket holder David for lending me one of his season tickets so that I could cover the game for my book, just a shame for all concerned that Fulham lost, in the dying seconds too. Needless to say, my friend Julian was gutted 'we was robbed'.

Farmers' Market

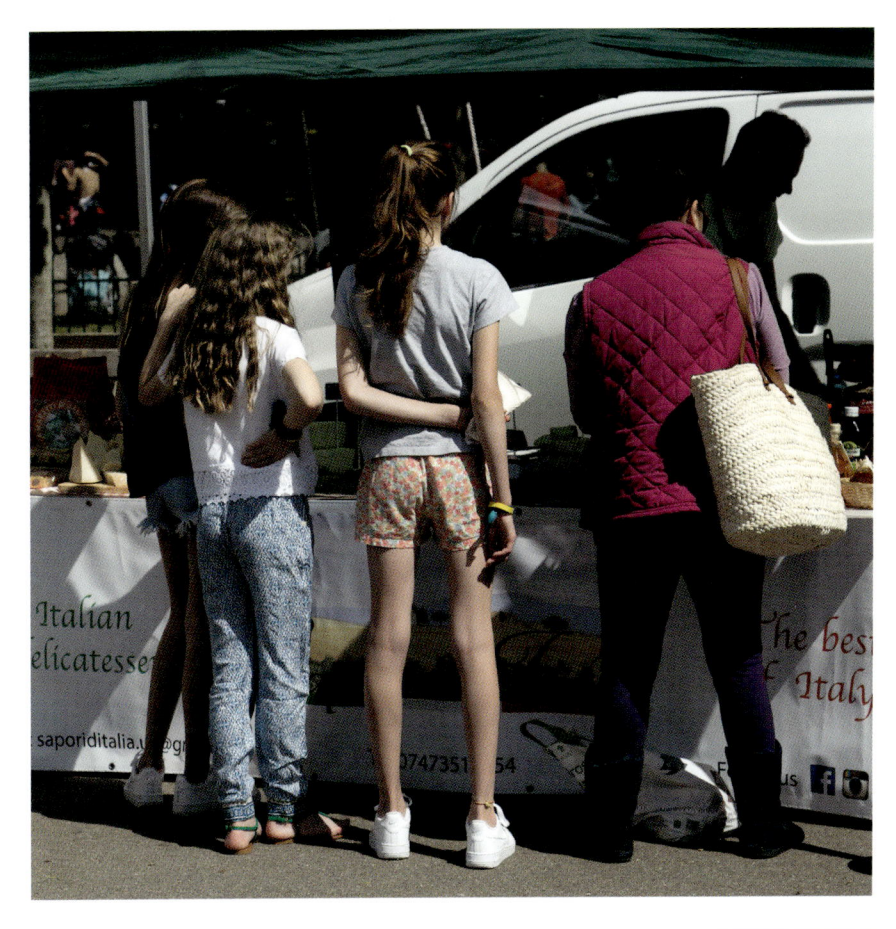

The Sunday Farmers' Market in Bishop's Park is run by RMS Markets. Offering a wide range of fresh produce it is well supported by the local community and visitors alike.

Alphabet Streets

A ladder of streets running between Stevenage Road and Fulham Palace Road near Bishop's Park are locally known as "The Alphabet Streets", each road's name starting with the next letter in the alphabet.

Below and opposite bottom right: Doneraile Street

Opposite bottom right: The trees appear to make a heart shape in the sky.

Opposite top: Many of the houses on Cloncurry Street retain the original tiling in their front porches.

Opposite centre left: Finlay Street

Opposite bottom left: Ellerby Street

55

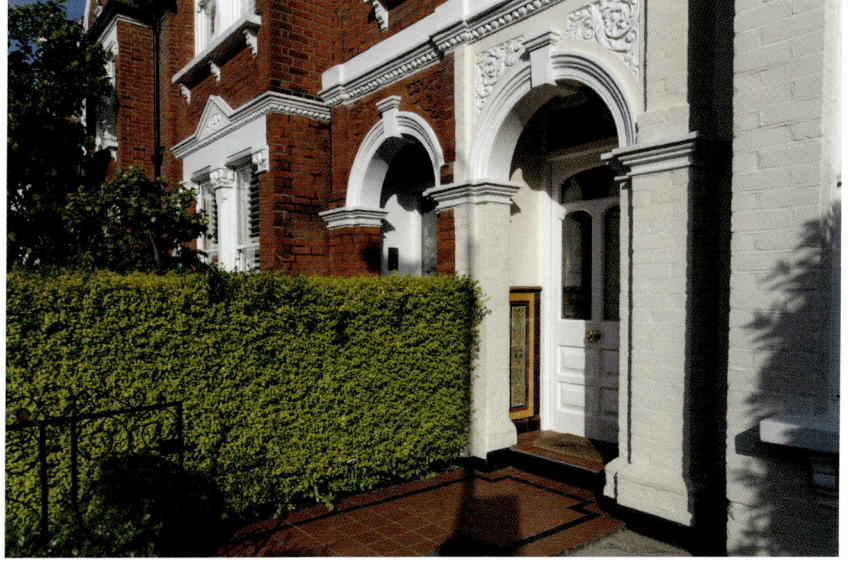

This page and bottom opposite: Bishops Park Tennis Centre, part of the Rocks Lane Multi Sports Centre group, is the newest club base in the group of three sports clubs that Chris and Liz Warren run, the others being on Chiswick Common in Chiswick and their original club at Rocks Lane across the river in Barnes.

Opposite top: Fulham Palace Road

57

Riverside Walk to the Crabtree Pub

Besides our main walks (on pages 68 and 74) this walk along the river to the Crabtree Pub has become a personal favourite of mine whilst working on this book. There are some exciting plans for the walk as Fulham Football Club intend on building a new stand. A new path will pass right beneath the stand meaning you will not have to walk around the stadium to follow the riverside path beyond the football ground. The riverside village of Crabtree took its name from the large crabtree growing by the inn. The first pub was known in the 1760s as The Pot House after a nearby pottery, later changing its name to The Three Jolly Gardeners as it became the place for labourers from surrounding market gardens to quench their thirst and finally taking the name of the village itself.

Top right and left: The seating area at the end of the path in Bishop's Park beside Craven Cottage is a particular favourite spot come the end of the day.

Bottom: The view from The Crabtree

Right and opposite page:
Tucked between Craven Cottage, the oldest football stadium in London, and a recent apartment complex is the sliver of Stevenage Park with its frontage on to the river.

Overleaf: The remains of a timber loading platform used by the Anglo-American Oil Company's depot at Dorset Wharf is a reminder of the many wharves along Fulham Reach which were used by factories and warehouses.

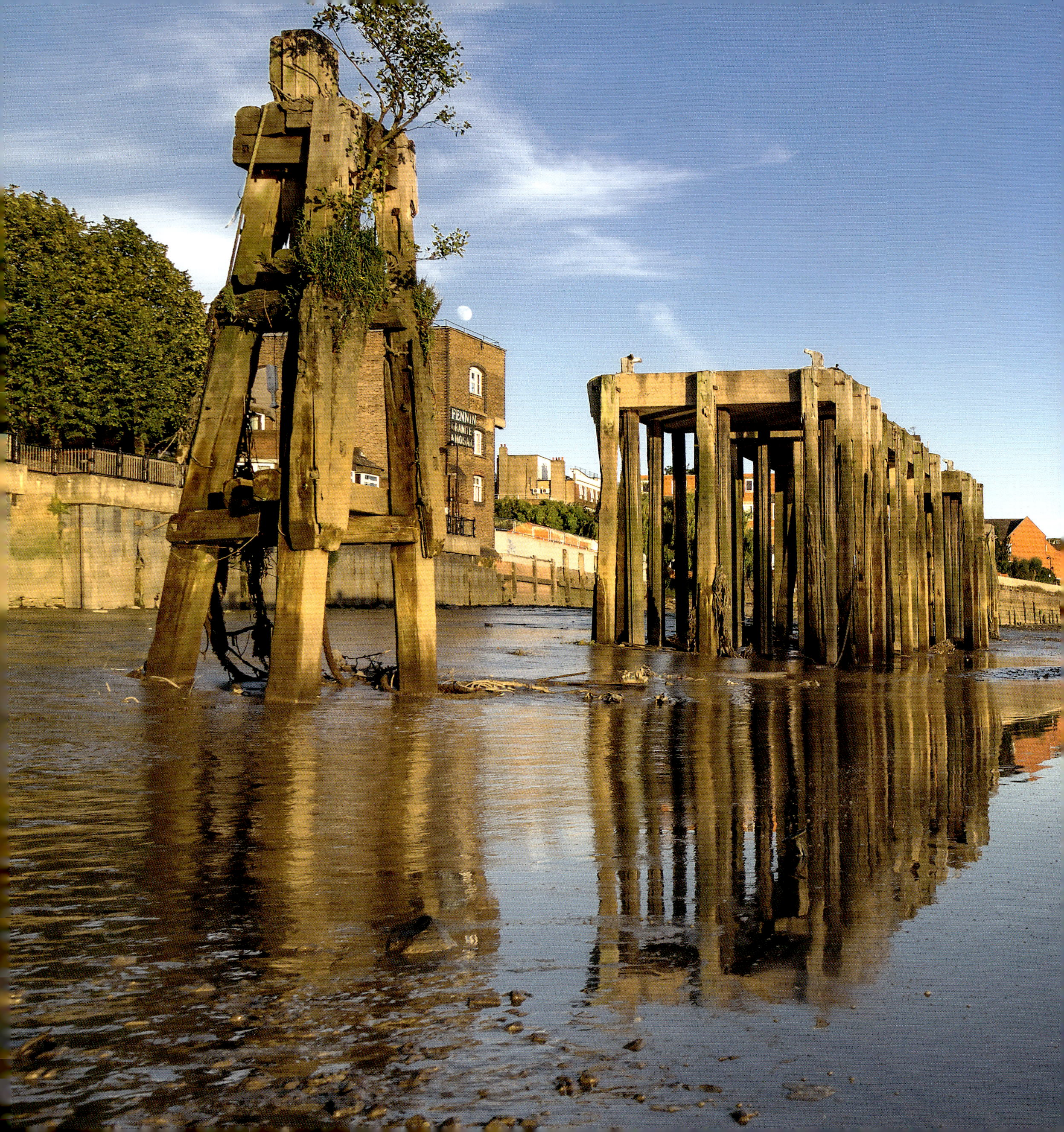

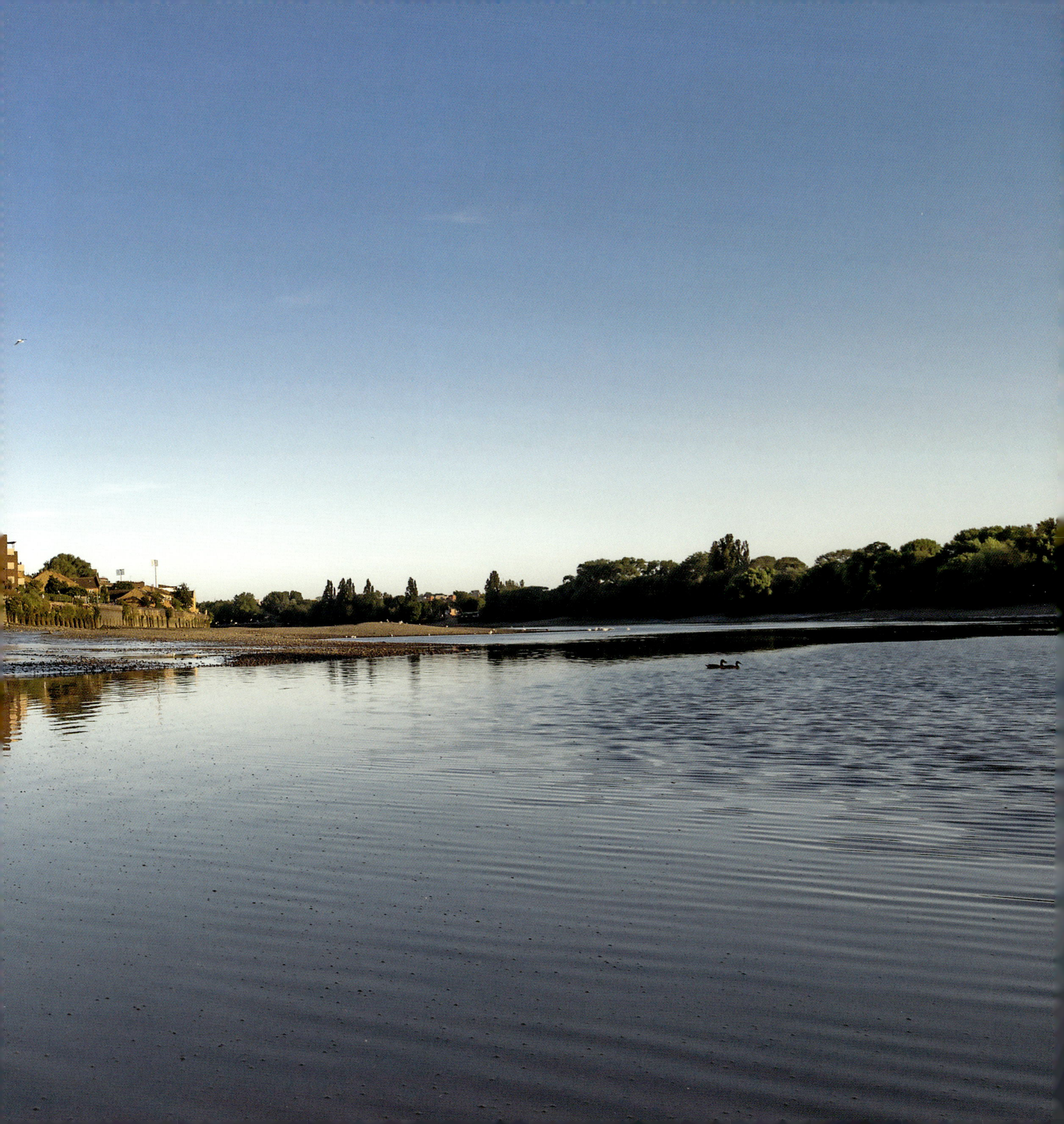

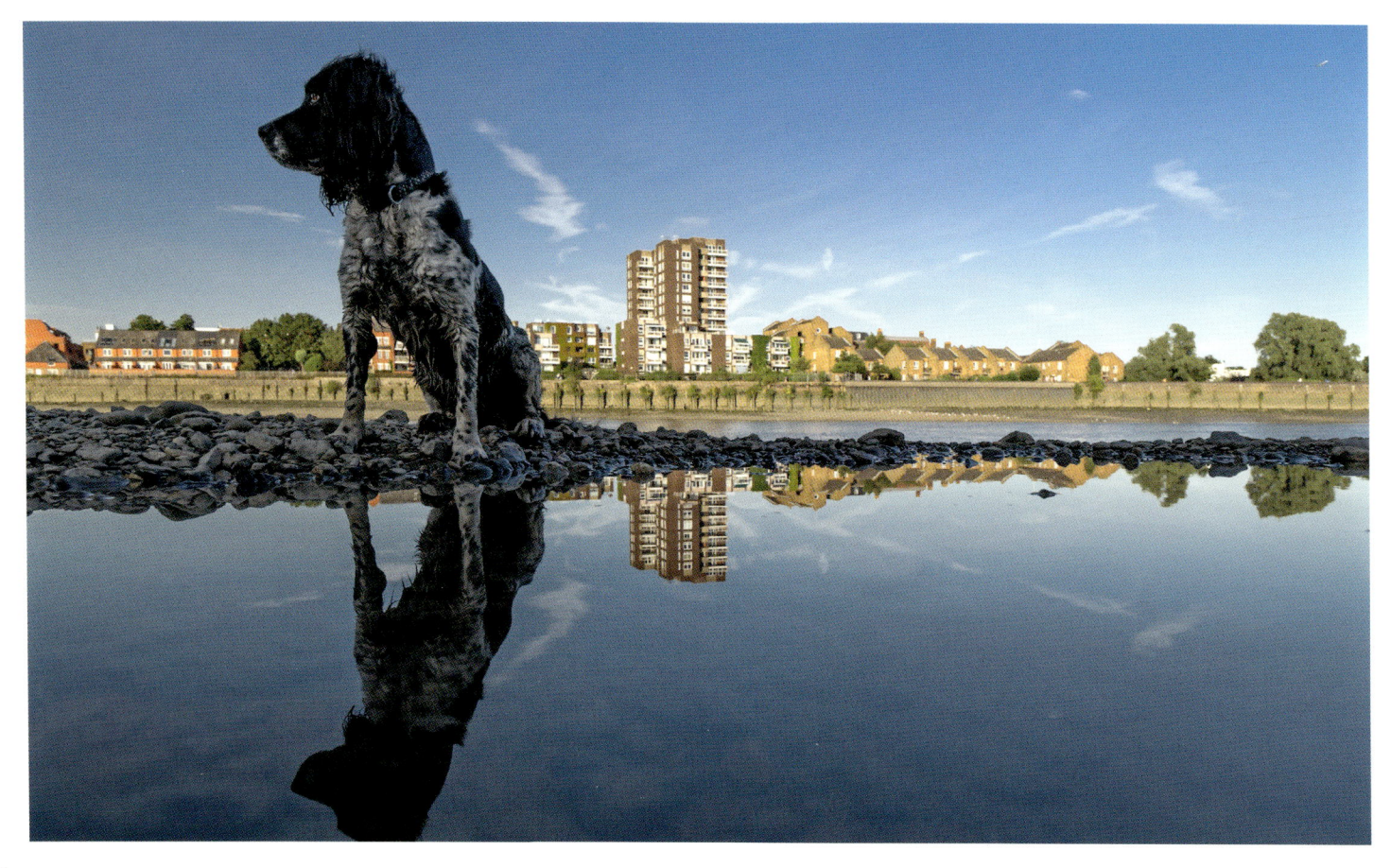

Rowberry Mead is the site of an old homestead dating back to 1638. The adjoining cherry orchard was reputed to be "the finest in England".

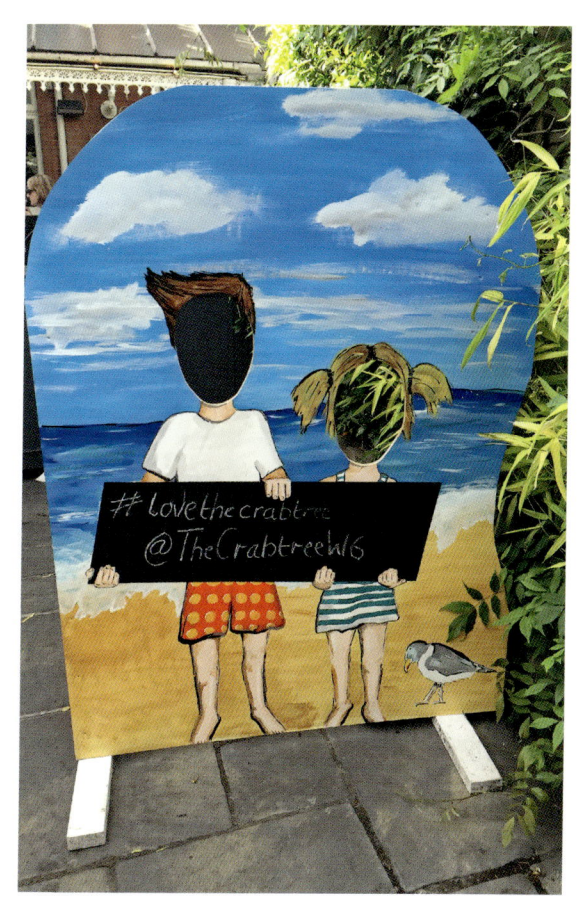

The Red Valerians lining part of the riverside walk in May and June are a delight.

Street Scenes

Whilst Fulham High Street was once the heart of the 18th century village of Fulanham it is now a busy thoroughfare of traffic coming and going across Putney Bridge. But step into secluded Church Gate and you are transported back in time by the almshouses and their delightful gardens. Fulham is full of surprises, walk from its Palace to enjoy a drink at the Crabtree and you can count the 'alphabet streets' which run between Fulham Palace Road to the river. Peterborough, Broomhouse, Hurlingham and Lillie Roads all remind us that this once rural area attracted gentry who established extensive estates within easy reach of the city of London. But with the need for more housing as London continued to spread westwards these estates were sold to developers such as Jimmy Nichols whose houses with their trademark terracotta lions on the former Peterborough estate went on sale in 1888 for £300.

The opening of Walham Green station in 1880 – later renamed Fulham Broadway – opened up the area which has since become a vibrant centre of commercial and social activity. It is the Sands End of Fulham where the greatest street changes are found. Sandford Manor, reputed to have been the home of Nell Gwynn, Charles II's favourite mistress, is now hidden behind high walls, Imperial Square with its Victorian houses remains intact but the vast area formerly occupied by the gas works is rapidly being covered with new homes. The paper mills, laundries and factories of Townmead Road making biscuits and beer have long since closed and together with the riverside warehouses been replaced by modern apartment blocks, restaurants and supermarkets, thus bringing new life to this part of Fulham.

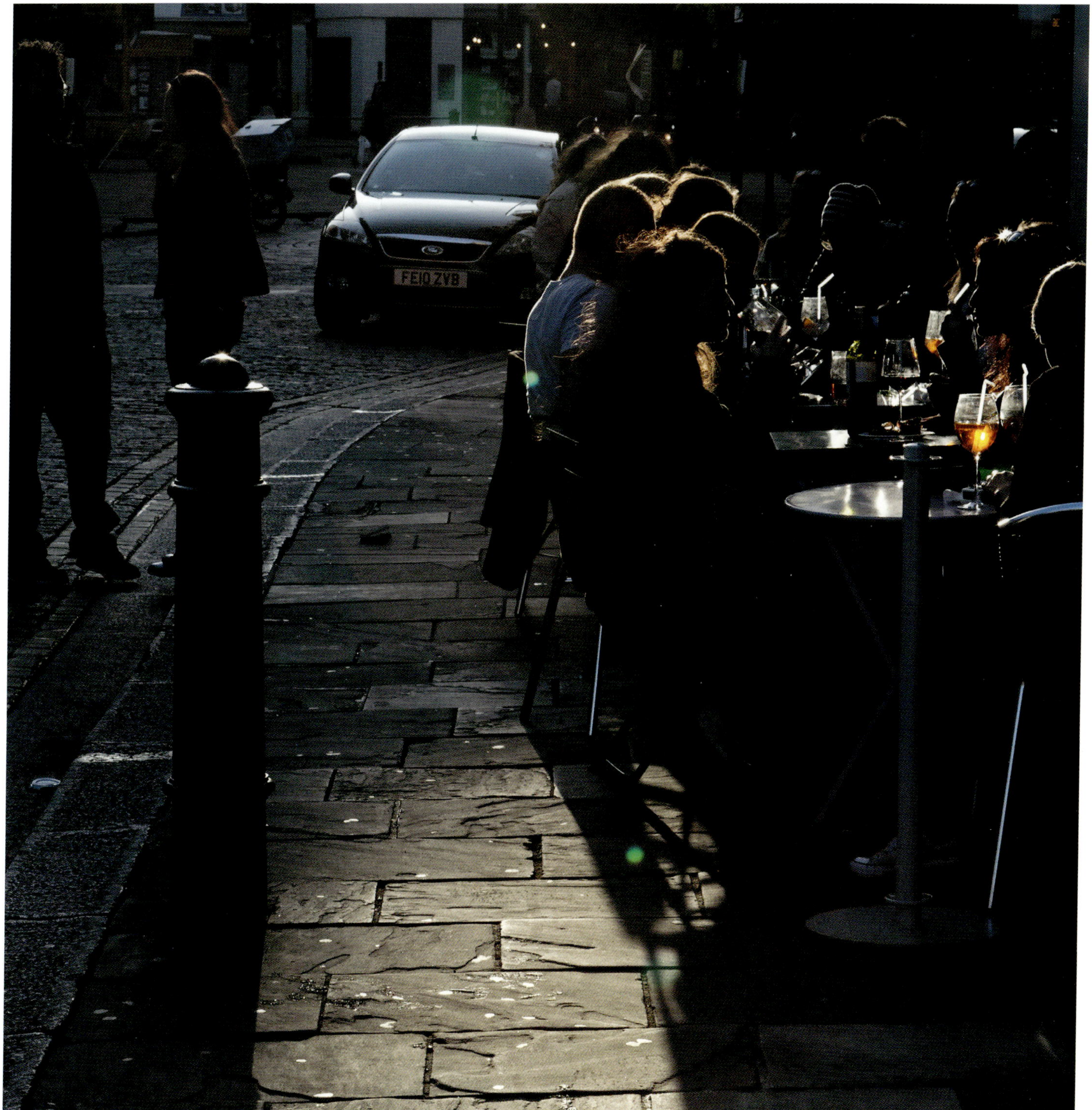
FE10 ZVB

A stroll around Sands End

Time: 1hr 15 mins

Exiting Fulham Broadway station (1), turn left into Fulham Road and just a few steps away is the modern church for the Methodists who have worshipped on this site for nearly two hundred years, the current unique glass entrance was unveiled for the 2000 Millennium. Just a little further along is the Sir Oswald Stoll Foundation, established by theatrical impresario Sir Oswald Stoll in 1916 to provide comfortable and inexpensive homes for servicemen injured in World War I. On the gate is a list of the famous battles of that war and if you step inside there is a fascinating plaque displaying the names of donors to this project. (2 and 3) Across the road the Lord Roberts Memorial Workshops and factory were established in Waterford Road, it is now a private development but its history is recorded on the wall of the new building.

Just past the gate to Chelsea's football ground there are two wooden doors, one with impressive lion handles, which lead to Chelsea Studios (4), a private hidden village of red tiled houses which overlook garden courtyards and archwayed paths. Cross Fulham Road carefully at the controlled pedestrian lights, the Butcher's Hook pub (5) to your left is famous for a historical moment in sporting history as over 100 years ago in what was then the Rising Sun, a handshake between founding directors marked the formation of Chelsea Football Club.

© Googlemaps 2015

Head down Holmead Road into King's Road and after using the pedestrian crossing to your right turn into Cambria Street. You are now on the former estate of Sandford Manor, originally built in the late 17th century and reputed to have been the residence of Nell Gwynn, favourite mistress to King Charles II, but what remains of the Grade II listed house is hard to see as it hides behind high walls, mature trees and modern developments.

Head along industrial Michael Road to the tumble down looking Art Bronze Foundry (8), one of the oldest foundries in London having been established in 1922 and over the years has produced bronze castings for many great sculptors including Henry Moore and Elizabeth Frink. Opposite the foundry you pass the Harley Davidson showroom (6). On the corner of Waterford Road is the now closed and sadly dilapidated frontage of a former pub and restaurant with its colourful glass windows and ornately carved front door (9).

Walk slowly and take the narrow un-named alley on your left between two more recent houses and so into Imperial Square (7) with its charming terraced houses set round an open area still lit by the original Victorian lamps. Built in the 1860s for workers of the nearby Imperial Gas Company it is locally known as German Square as it also housed German workers brought over when local workers went on strike. Leaving the square at the south end, short Emden Street is a reminder of the port from which those Germans sailed from their country. As you turn left into Imperial Road looming ahead is the oldest known gasholder in the world, built in 1830 and now a listed building (10).

Bear right into Fulmead Street – at the end the large building on the corner of Pearscroft Road was the Queen Elizabeth pub (13) now transformed into a youth hostel – but turn left down Bagley's Lane so named after the family who owned extensive market gardens in the area, 35 acres of which were given to fruit and nut trees. Turn right into Stephendale Road (11 and 15) where imposing Grove House, now a nursery school, stands on one corner with the more recent housing of Stanford Court on the other.

The current Grove House is a nineteenth century rebuild of a much earlier residence which was occupied by four generations of the Smith family, all with the Christian name of Deliverance. Just off Stephendale Road you will find the delightful William Parnell Park (12), also known as Pineapple Park on account of the sculpture found there (see introduction on page 4).

71

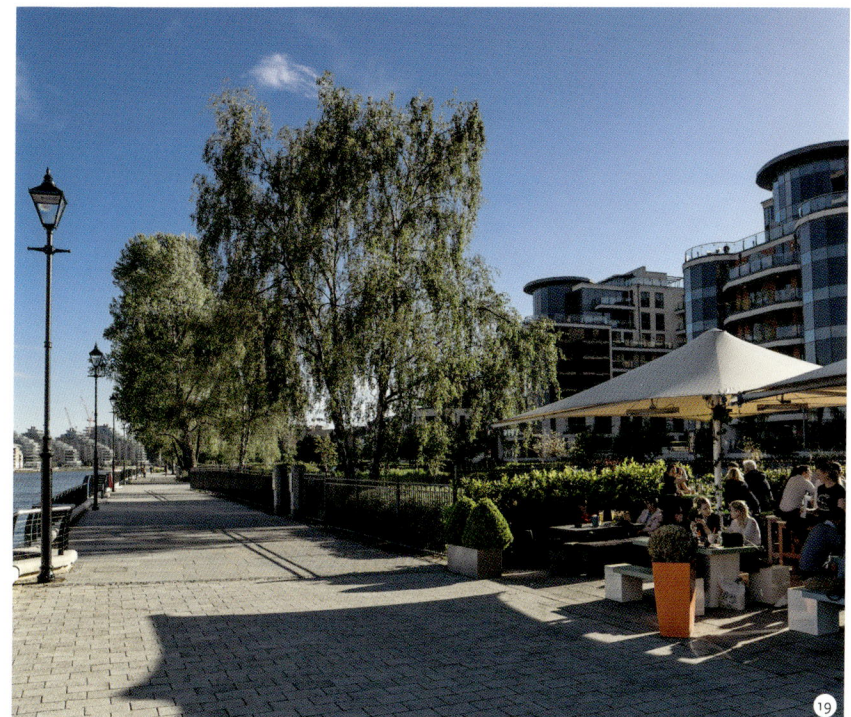

Follow the road as it bears left and at the bend by the church go straight down Tynemouth Street and finally in to Imperial Park (18 and 19), created in 2009 as part of the regeneration of the Sands End industrial area. Enjoy the view of the river with ever soaring upwards residential developments across the water and follow the Thames Path (14, 16 and 17) to your right until it eventually turns inland again and meets Townmead Road. Go left but stop to read the blue plaque on the former building of Kops Brewery (25 and 26) which in 1893 covered an eight acre site and produced a non-alcoholic beer, it subsequently became a margarine factory.

At the busy junction with Wandsworth Bridge, cross carefully and head right just a short way up Wandsworth Bridge Road before bearing left into Hugon Road (22). Thomas's Preparatory School is accommodated in a building which opened in 1894 to educate 1200 local boys and girls. Walk through South Park, something which the public have enjoyed since 1904 thanks to local benefactress Miss Charlotte Sulivan.

Prior to that it was part of the Southfield and Broom House Farms which finally became famous market gardens run by the Rench family who introduced many new species to this country including Auriculas. At Clancarty Road turn left and then right into Peterborough Road (23), if you peer down Studdridge Street you will spot some of Jimmy Nichols' famous lion houses (20).

Cross New King's Road and enjoy another of Fulham's open spaces, Parsons Green (21), which derives its name from when it was owned by the local rector. In the early 18th century this was considered the most aristocratic part of Fulham and according to early historian John Bowack "inhabited mostly by gentry and persons of quality". Mrs Fitzherbert, mistress and for a while 'secret wife' of the Prince of Wales, lived at East End House whilst his brother, the Duke of Clarence, accommodated his mistress, Mrs Jordan, at Belfield House which is now part of the Lady Margaret School. The White Horse (28), affectionately known locally as The Sloaney Pony has served ale since the late 18th century so why not rest your feet here and take refreshment as Parsons Green tube station is just a short way up Green Lane.

Walk devised by
Caroline MacMillan
www.westlondonwalks.co.uk

A walk around Fulham

Time: 1hr

Starting at Fulham Broadway tube station which was known as Walham Green when it opened in 1880 and with the Victorian classical renaissance style former Town Hall opposite (1) turn right, cross the road at the traffic lights and continue down Harwood Road. Cross at the pelican lights and into Kempson Road and then left down the slope on to Eel Brook Common (2), it's name derives from Helbroke or 'hill brook' and for centuries it was a very marshy common. Follow the path beside the wall for a few yards and then take the path which forks right and continue over the common to the New King's Road.

Cross at the lights, turn right and admire the Talisman Art Deco building (3) which was built in the 1930s as a garage and further along the delightful Pomona House which contains some wonderful artist studios. By turning left into Perrymead Street – the name reminds us that orchards once covered this area – you have now entered Jimmy Nichols' lion country (4, 5 and 6), they peer down from every house, go right into Studdridge Street (yet more lions) and finally left at Peterborough Road.

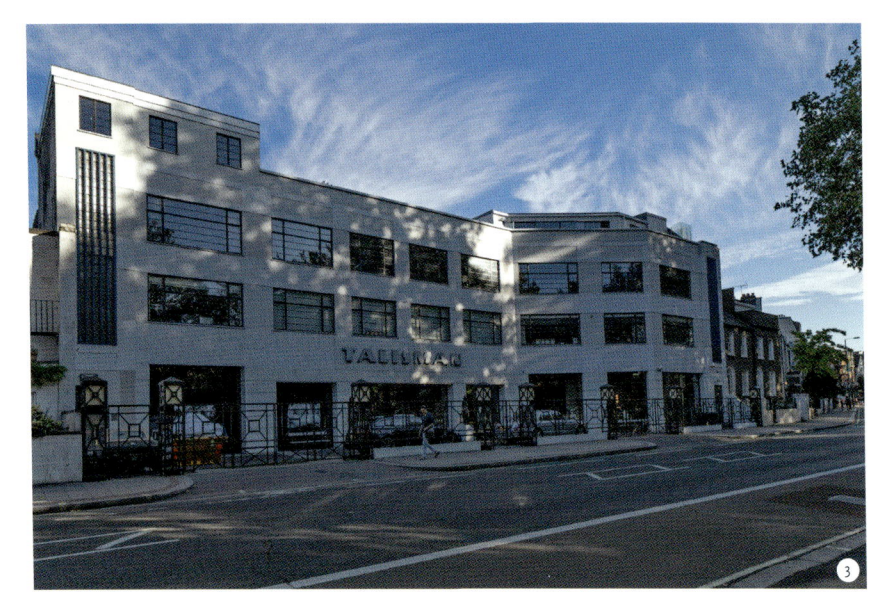

© Googlemaps 2015

Sulivan Court (7) is a post-war housing estate built on the site of one of the exclusive Hurlingham Club's polo field whilst South Park on the left was part of the Veitch family's extensive nursery gardens and opened as a public park in 1904 thanks to local benefactress Miss Charlotte Sulivan. Keep following the park's brick wall until you reach Sulivan Road (8) where you turn right. The early 20th century terraced houses are known locally as "the footballers' houses" as they were built by the Mears brothers, founders of Chelsea Football Club, as a perk for the players of their modestly paid team.

Go right into Broomhouse Lane which once led to a farm of the same name. The splendid Tudor-Gothic building was formerly the Elizabethan School (9) but is now a private residence. At Hurlingham Road glance to the right and admire Broom Villa (10) which dates back to 1718 and was recently for sale for £5m. Along this route there are roads which lead off Hurlingham Lane which are worth a look (pictures 11–16). Enjoy for free the open space of Hurlingham Park and read its history on a board at the entrance gate. The Vineyard (17), a lovely house on the opposite side of the road was once home to Lord Beaverbrook the formidable business tycoon, politician and newspaper proprietor and is a reminder of the splendid houses which once graced Fulham.

77

This Page and Previous Page: Linver (11, 12 and 13) and Alderville Road's (14, 15 and 16), off Hurlingham Road, which you will pass on the walk can look great in the spring, especially when the blossom is out.

Approaching the New King's Road, Charles Ivey's extensive garage (18) across the road was formerly a baker's premises whilst ahead is the restored kiln of The Fulham Pottery (20) which has been on this site for over 300 years. Bear left at the junction of Fulham High Street, cross at the lights by The Temperance (19), built as a billiard hall and as its name implies, served no alcohol.

Turn left and immediately right into Church Gate. Egmont Villa was home to Granville Sharpe, one of the first English campaigners for the abolition of the slave trade, you will find his tomb in the nearby grave yard. The delightful William Powell almshouses (21 and 22) have been on this site since 1869 and were brought up to modern standards very recently.

Ahead is All Saints Church (23), a place of worship since the 12th century. Follow the path past the church, through the gate and into Bishop's Park, the land being a gift to the public from the Ecclesiastical Commissioners.

Almost immediately there is an entrance into the grounds of Fulham Palace, follow the arrow saying 'Main Entrance' then through the door in the wall which leads you into The Walled Garden (23, 25 and 26) with its wonderfully restored glass houses and exit via the original Tudor doorway on to the lawns of Fulham Palace. Until 1973 it was the country home of the Bishop of London and is now a museum with an excellent shop and cafe.

After your visit retrace your steps to Fulham High Street and follow the signs for Putney Bridge underground station (27).

This sculpture (24) can be seen on the approach to Putney Bridge before turning off towards the station.

Walk devised by Caroline MacMillan.
www.westlondonwalks.co.uk

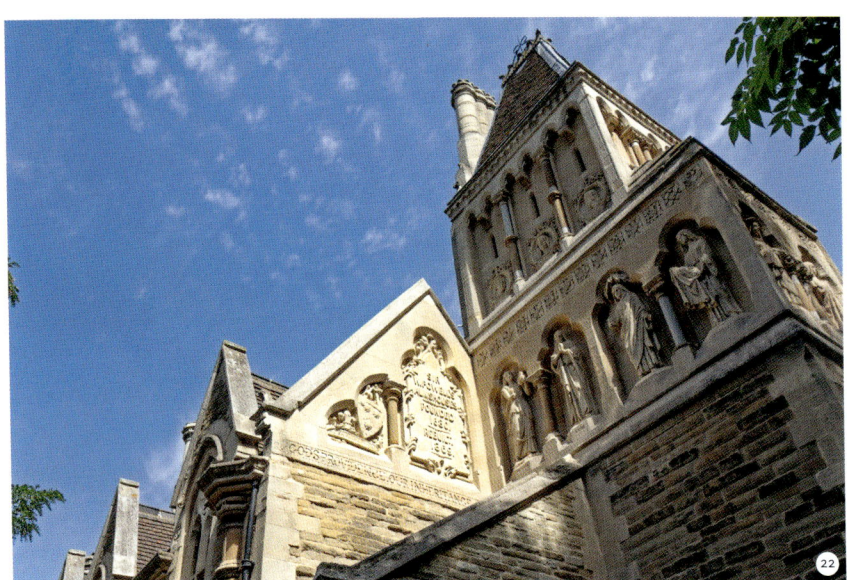

81

Fulham Broadway

Once upon a time in the 17th century in Fulham there was a hamlet called Walham Green complete with manor house and village pond. The hamlet became a village which in turn became part of spreading London so when the Metropolitan District Railway extended its line in 1880 the local station was called Walham Green. But a disappearing act began in 1952 when the station was renamed Fulham Broadway. So the old name went into decline and the area became known as Fulham Broadway. The only reminder of that little hamlet is a nearby street called Walham Grove.

Top left and opposite: Clarion sculpture by British designer Phillip King stands in the centre of Fulham Broadway.

Bottom left: The former Red Lion, now named The Slug at Fulham retains the original lion statue on its roof.

Bottom right: El Metro traditional tapas restaurant, with its delightful artwork, just off Harwood Road in Effie Road.

Top right: The rather magnificent, almost art deco building, home to M&S Simply Food.

Inset: Jerdan Place

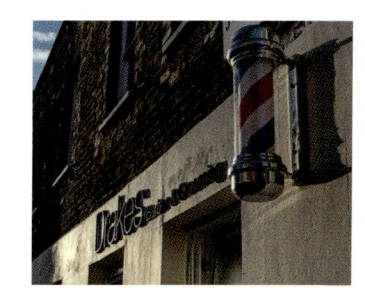

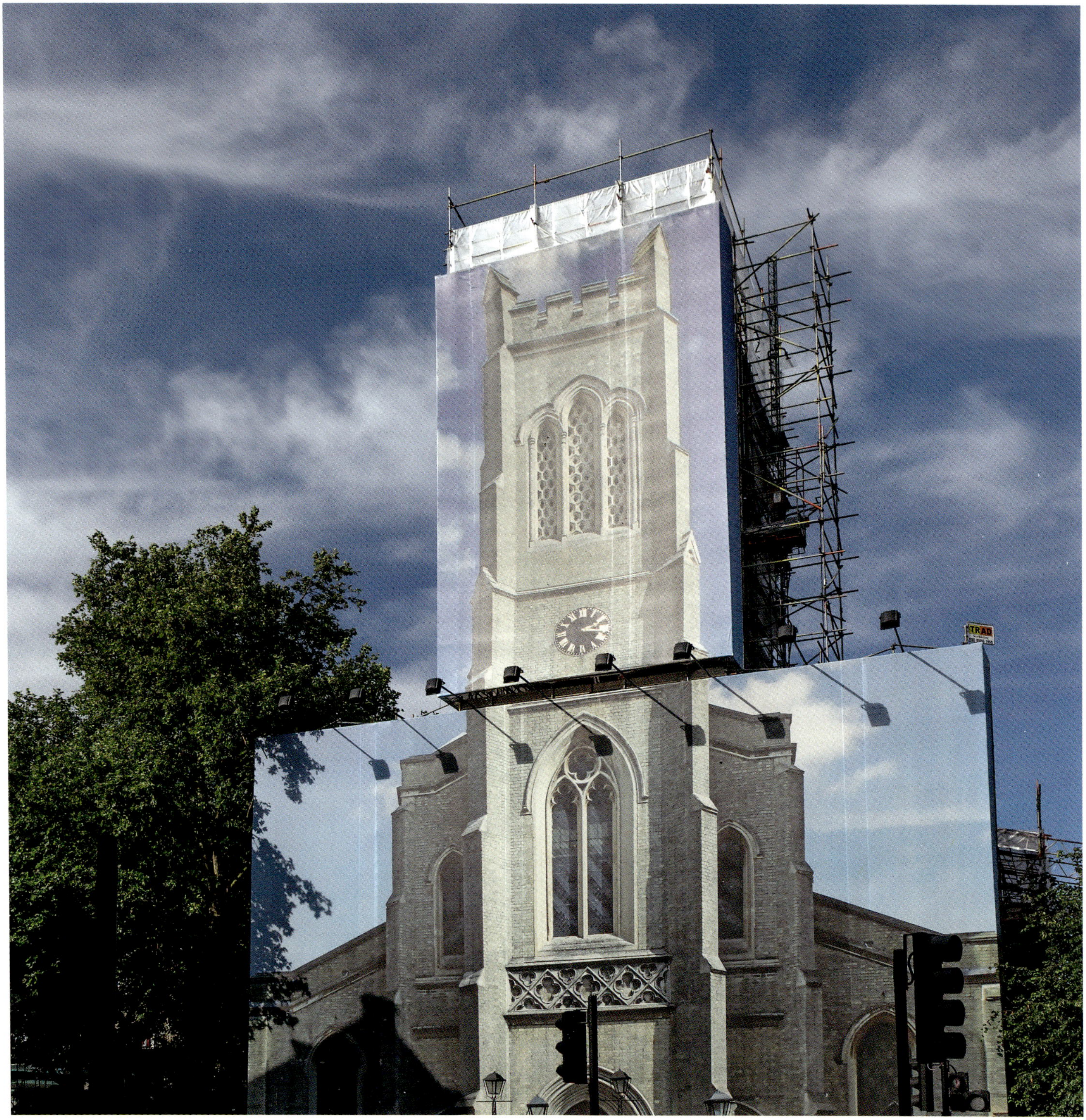

Opposite: St John's Church on North End Road, currently under reconstruction.

Top right: The former Walham Green Station entrance became redundant in 2003.

Top left: The Broadway Bar and Grill, formerly The Kings Head. Above the bar is a private club, Broadway House, with a fabulous roof garden (inset).

Bottom left: Jerdan Place was originally known as Market Place due to a flourishing market which served the surrounding area of Walham Green. At its peak the market stretched from Fulham Broadway right up to Hammersmith Road.

Bottom right: A pub has been on the site of the Malt House since 1729 when it was called The Maltster due to the locals working in the local brewing industry. In 1890 residents of Farm Lane petitioned for their cobbled street to be paved with wood owing to the noise from the horses that pulled the buses and stabled in the lane.

Fulham Road

Below: Fulham Library opened in 1909, paid for by Andrew Carnegie, the Scots born American industrialist who had benefited from using libraries in his youth and gave large sums to build libraries throughout the country. Next to the library can be found Kensington Prep School, which throughout the summer of 2015 was under scaffolding whilst undergoing some renovation.

Opposite top left: A unique sight – Fulham Road with next to no traffic, this rare occurrence happened when Putney Bridge was closed for repair.

Opposite right column: Nomad Bookshop was opened 25 years ago by Harriet Morton who still runs the shop alongside staff Tara and Isabel (bottom). She also designed the charming figures which run around the top of the shop building (top).

Inset left: The wheatsheaf ornamental flourish above Sainsbury's is a reminder of the pub which used to host this site. The Wheatsheaf pub closed in 2012.

Bottom left: The bright display of lamps in Best and Lloyd, an interior shop on Fulham Road.

Top left: There is a wonderful display of blossom along Waldemer Avenue in spring.

Top right: The first fire station was replaced in 1895 by this splendid building which contained living quarters for the firemen and stables for horses. Prior to this fire-fighting was undertaken by individual fire insurance companies and insured properties carried a metal firemark on the front of the house.

Bottom left: Officially a picture framing shop, Artsbeat also has a great selection of Fulham memorabilia.

Bottom right: As well as gifts, Indian Summers also sells clothes. Owner Ruth Green opened the shop in 2004 and since then it has been listed in Vogue Magazine's 100 greatest shops – "the secret addresses you must remember".

Opposite page: You will often hear live music coming from the Durell Arms on the junction of Munster Road.

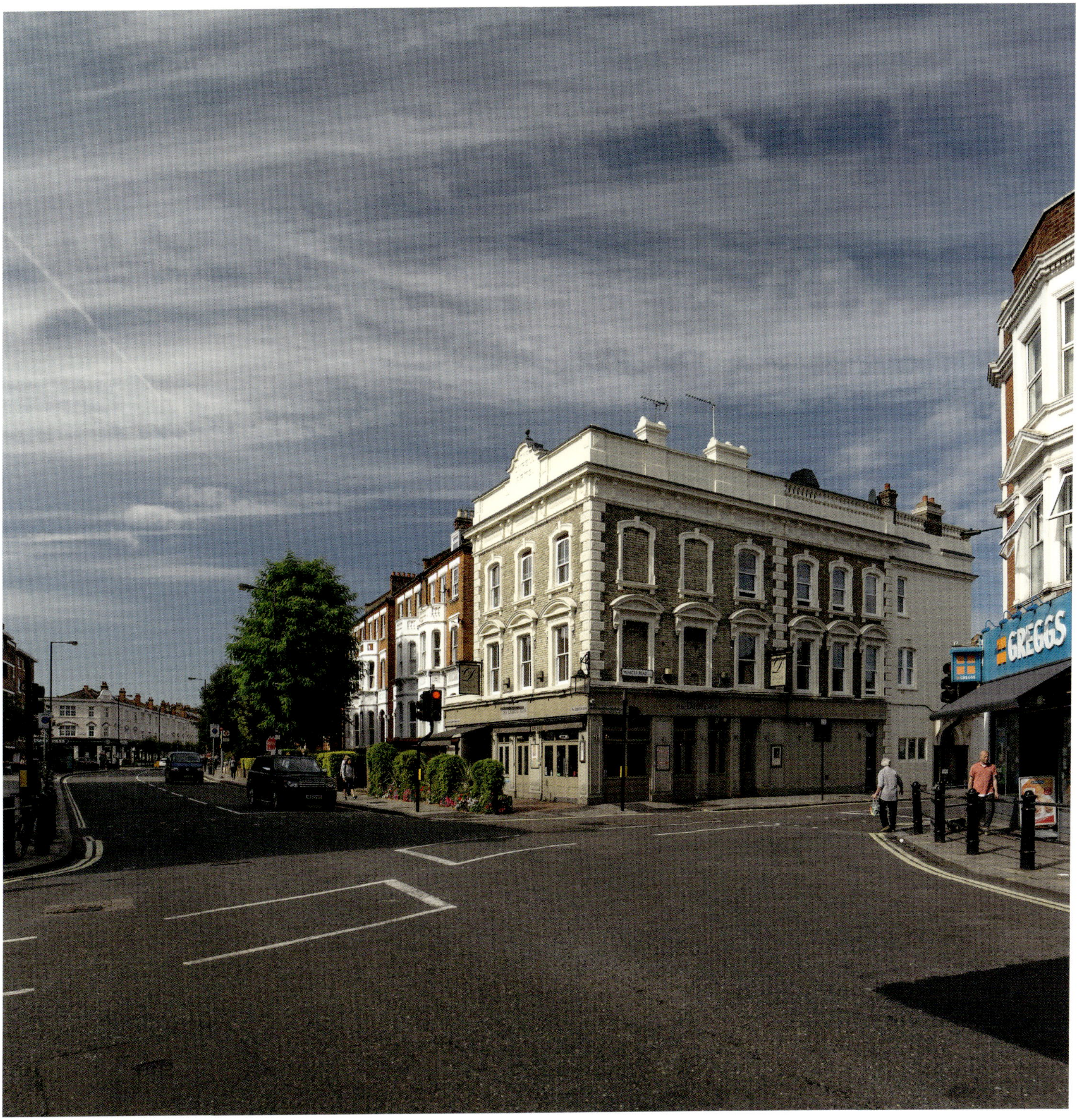
GREGGS

Munster Road

This page: The impressive St John's Walham Green CE Primary School was founded in 1836 and moved to its current location in 1997. We rather liked this original sign found on one of the outside walls.

Top left: A 110 years ago Batey and Company's Mineral Water Works occupied the site where Coda Studios now stand.

Below: Fulham Cross Girls School is a member of the Mayor's London Schools' Gold Club and the only girls' school in the Fulham College Federation.

Bottom left: Painted signs on walls were a common form of advertising in the late 19th century. This hand-painted sign is a reminder of the shop's history.

Munster House, a mansion with Tudor origins set in eight acres was demolished in 1895, now only the road reminds us of its existence.

Left: Originally opening in 1898, Kingswood School later formed part of Henry Compton School, its name commemorating the Bishop of London who beautified the grounds of Fulham Palace. The school now goes by the name of Fulham College Boys' School. As well as a playground there is also this rather magnificent building, partially obscured by other buildings and houses, hence the rather jaunty angle and slight blurriness, as the picture had to be taken through a window. Thank you to Linda Potter for showing me around.

Opposite top right: Italian restaurant Locale with its bright awning that coincidentally matches next door's truck!

Opposite top left and bottom: Luna Stein's Florist shop is a treasure trove of blooms including stunning tropical flowers from South America and her native South Africa.

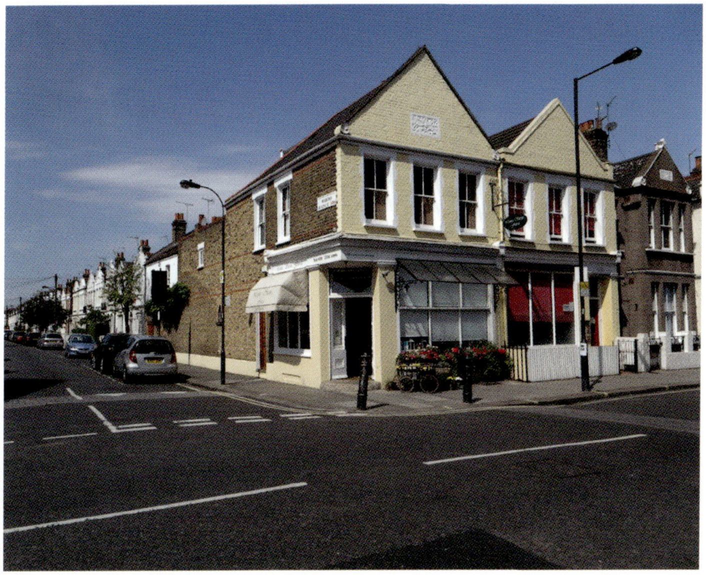

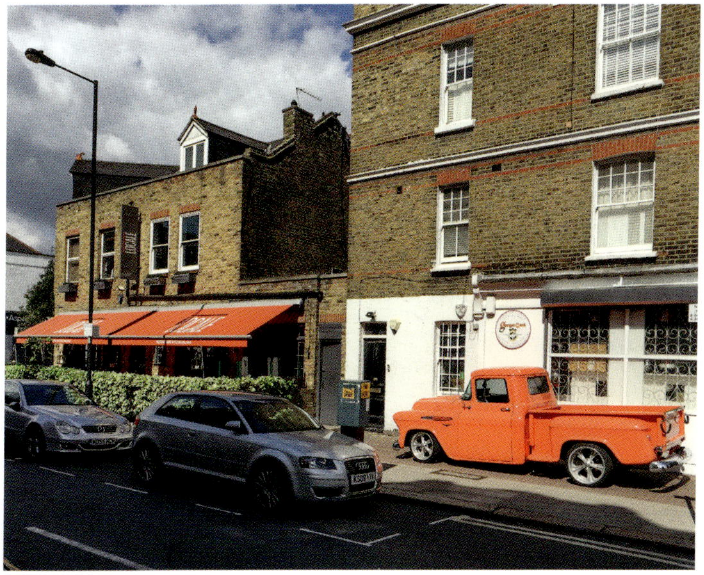

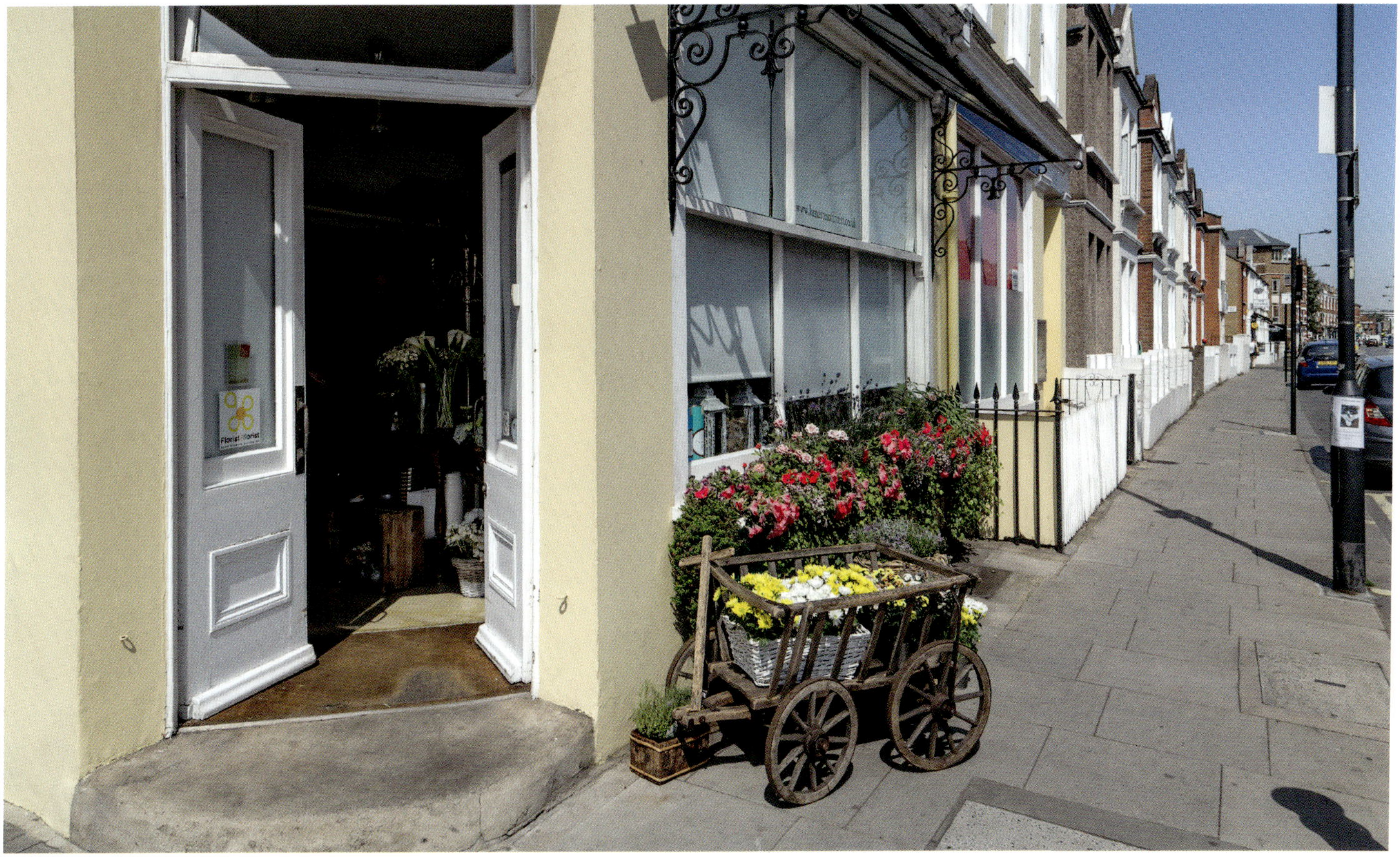

New King's Road

Opposite: New King's Road was originally a private road for the sole use of the Monarch. It opened to the general public in 1830.

Top right: Besides selling presents, Gifts on the Green has a huge range of candles and candle accessories.

Bottom right: John Dwight established his pottery in Fulham in 1684 and it remained in the family until 1859. The factory finally moved over the river to Battersea where it continues to produce pottery bearing the distinctive Fulham mark.

Inset: Mr Resistor has been selling lights in New King's Road since 1968.

Top and bottom left: Grafton and Koch gentlemen's grooming club, it is refreshing to see the traditional approach to hairdressing still being used.

The Parson's Green Farmers' Market takes place each Sunday on the playground of New Kings School in the New King's Road.

Bottom left: Will from the Channel Fish stall.

Bottom right: Liz on the Parsons Nose stall.

Bottom left opposite: Holli at the Aston's Bakery

97

North End Road

In late June the Summer Market is held on North End Road. The local council entirely pedestrianises the road and packs it with stalls on both sides up to Lillie Road.

Opposite bottom left: Ali hands out Turkish food; he is from the Best Mangal Restaurant just down the road in Fulham Road by the roundabout.

Opposite top right and inset: Paul and Ray Truss' fruit and veg stall has been a feature of the market for over 60 years having inherited it from their father Harry.

Opposite page bottom right: Hammersmith's Mayor, Mercy Umeh, her consort Mr Maxwell Umeh, her friend Shereen, Shereen's mum Anna, Alaska and Elijah enjoying the market.

This page: Super tall stilt walkers Zahara (pink) and Sarah (blue) roam the market amongst shoppers.

Opposite page bottom right: Halford Street is one of the few streets retaining its original Victorian railings. Most streets lost theirs in the last war when they were removed to be melted down for the war effort.

Opposite top and bottom left: The ultra modern design of the Rainsborough Square development is overlooked by the graceful 1893 Munster Road School. Thanks to Ola from JJ Homes for letting me in to take these pictures.

Bottom right and left: Clement Alexander with his tasty Caribbean food stall, a feature of the market most days.

101

Parsons Green

Once regarded as the most aristocratic part of Fulham, only a few of the handsome houses overlooking the green remain. One of the most famous residents of Elm House was Mrs Fitzherbert, mistress and later the secret wife of the Prince of Wales, the future King George IV. His brother the Duke of Clarence installed his mistress, Mrs Jordan, in Belfield House next door.

Top and bottom left: The Duke On The Green pub one of the only two left that were designed by sculptor Henry Poole in 1892. After undergoing an extensive refurbishment the Duke on the Green reopened in 2015.

Top right: Parsons Green Station opened in 1880 when the District Railway extended its line from West Brompton to Putney Bridge.

Bottom right: The Bayley and Sage store on Parsons Green, a charming traditional greengrocer with all the best seasonal fruit, vegetables, meat and cheese.

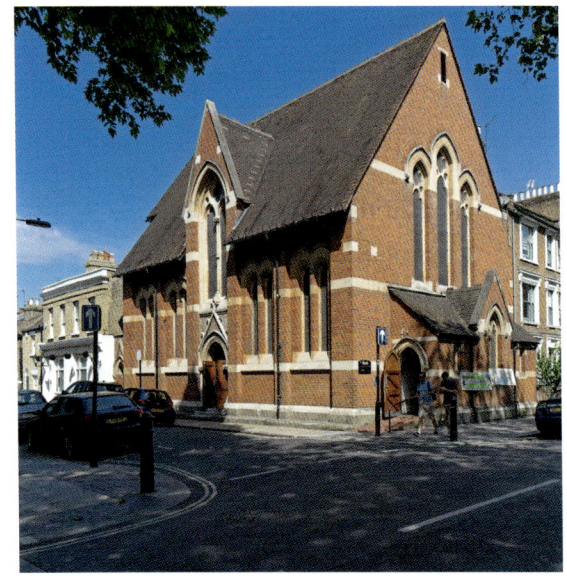

Left: St Dionis replaced an early church standing on the opposite corner of St Dionis Road which in turn became the Mission Hall. It was funded by the sale of St Dionis Backchurch, one of Sir Christopher Wren's redundant City churches which was demolished in 1878.

Bottom right: Parsons Green Lane

Top right and opposite: There has been a White Horse Inn overlooking the green since the early 18th century. A popular pub, it has been known for many years as 'The Sloaney Pony'.

THE WHITE HORSE
The WHITE HORSE On Parson's Green
THE WHITE HORSE
No 1
KEEP CLEAR CELLAR DOORS

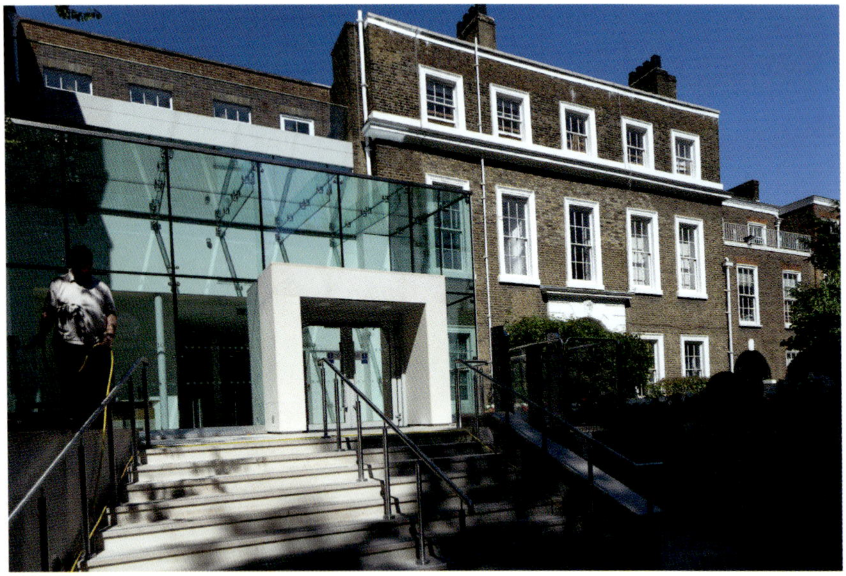

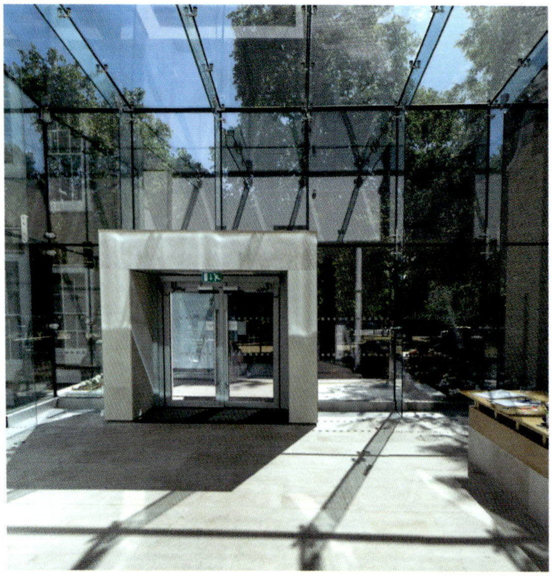

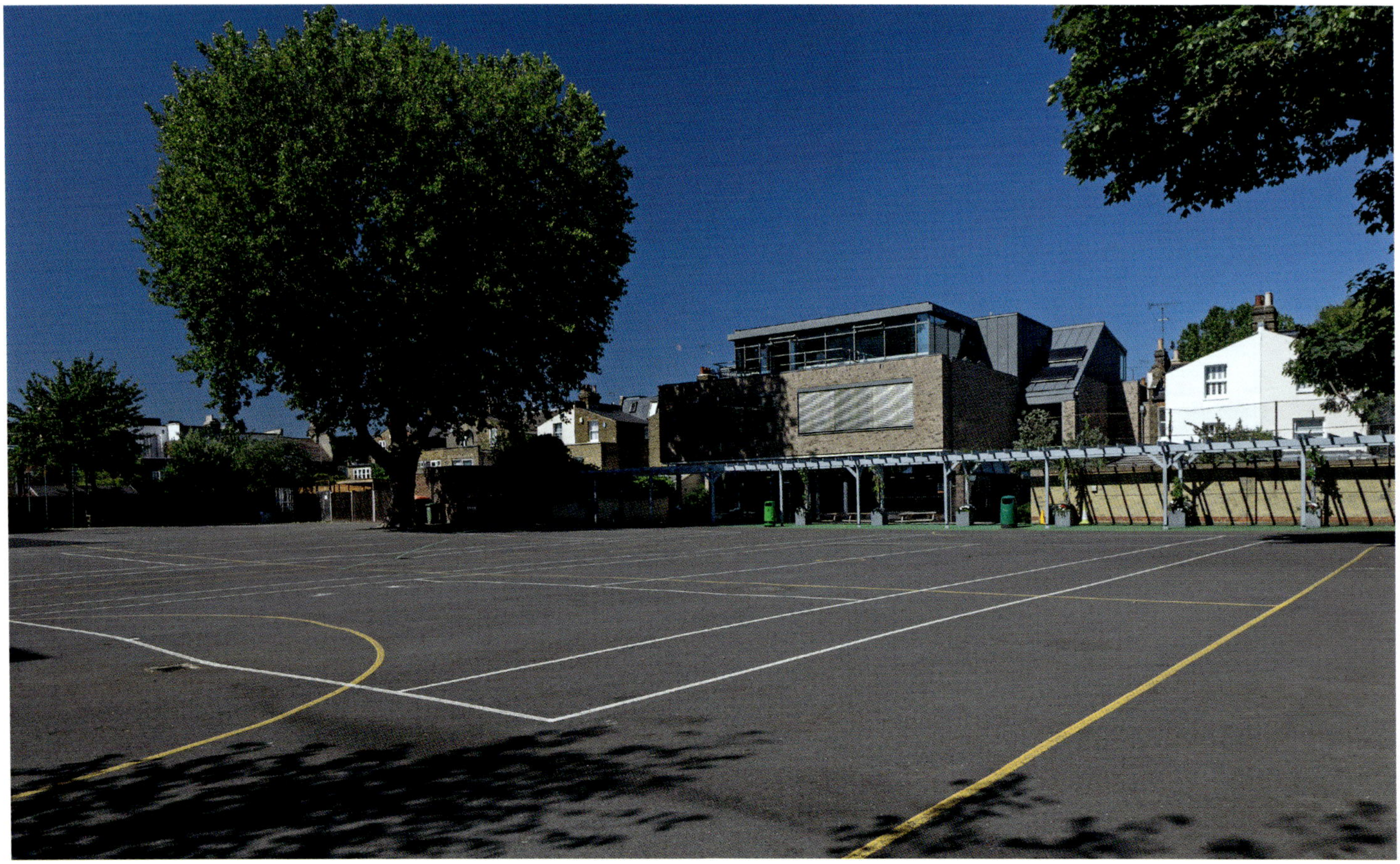

Lady Margaret School

Named after Lady Margaret Beaufort, mother of King Henry VII, Lady Margaret School opened in 1917 in formed Belfield House, twenty years later expanding into adjoining Elm House. Thank you to Libby for arranging my visit.

Parsons Green Fair

Opposite top right: Jane and Edna from the local history society on their stand. www.fhhs.org.uk

Established early in the 18th century for three days in August a fair was held on Parsons Green with a mixture of competitions, entertainment and stalls selling foods ranging from gingerbread to oysters.

The tradition ceased in 1820 when it was closed down as being deemed to be attracting 'undesirables'. The fair started up again over 21 years ago and has been held annually since then, each year becoming bigger and more popular.

Wandsworth Bridge Road

Opposite top left: I like the curve in Stokenchurch Street, off Wandsworth Bridge Road at the New King's Road end.

Opposite top right and bottom right: Visit John Rendell's Sophistocat Furniture and learn about a lion called Christian, which he bought as a cub from Harrods pet department in 1969.

Top left: The view of from Wandsworth Bridge Road looking south.

Bottom left: Randalls Butchers; it's nice to see that some butchers can continue in the traditional manner.

Top and bottom right: Ann May's furniture shop, which began life 60 years ago as a junk shop and is run by Mary Neave. Ann was her mum and she has been at the shop 47 of those years. She's seen quite a few changes in her time, for instance, when there was a book shop opposite.

Chelsea Football Club

Brothers Gus and Joseph Mears had long dreamed of establishing a football club and in 1904 they leased the site of the old London Athletic Club in Walham Green for their newly formed Chelsea Football Club – it has been their home ever since.

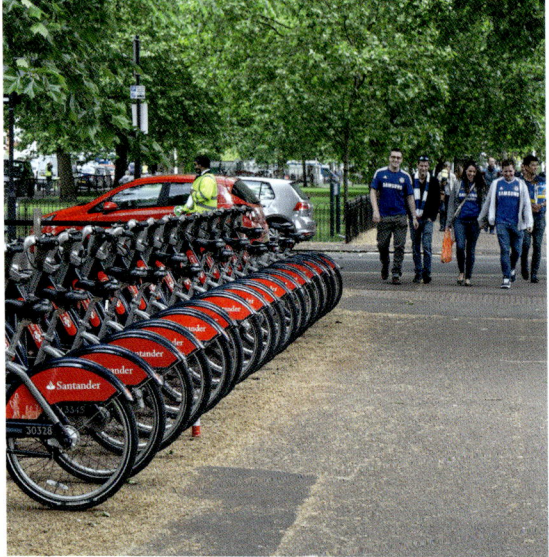

PETER OSGOOD

Opposite page left: Peter Osgood was one of their players from the '70s; something of a legend in Chelsea circles, Peter was a striker and played four times for England. He sadly died in 2006 when only 59.

Top right and bottom: The streets in Fulham are cleared for Chelsea's parade for winning the Premiership in 2015.

Inset: Thank you to my friend and fellow photographer Leonard, who lives in the New King's Road, for letting me take some pictures from his balcony.

Chelsea celebrate winning the Premiership in 2015 in the traditional manner with a parade through the streets of Fulham, here photographed as they pass down New King's Road opposite Eel Brook Common.

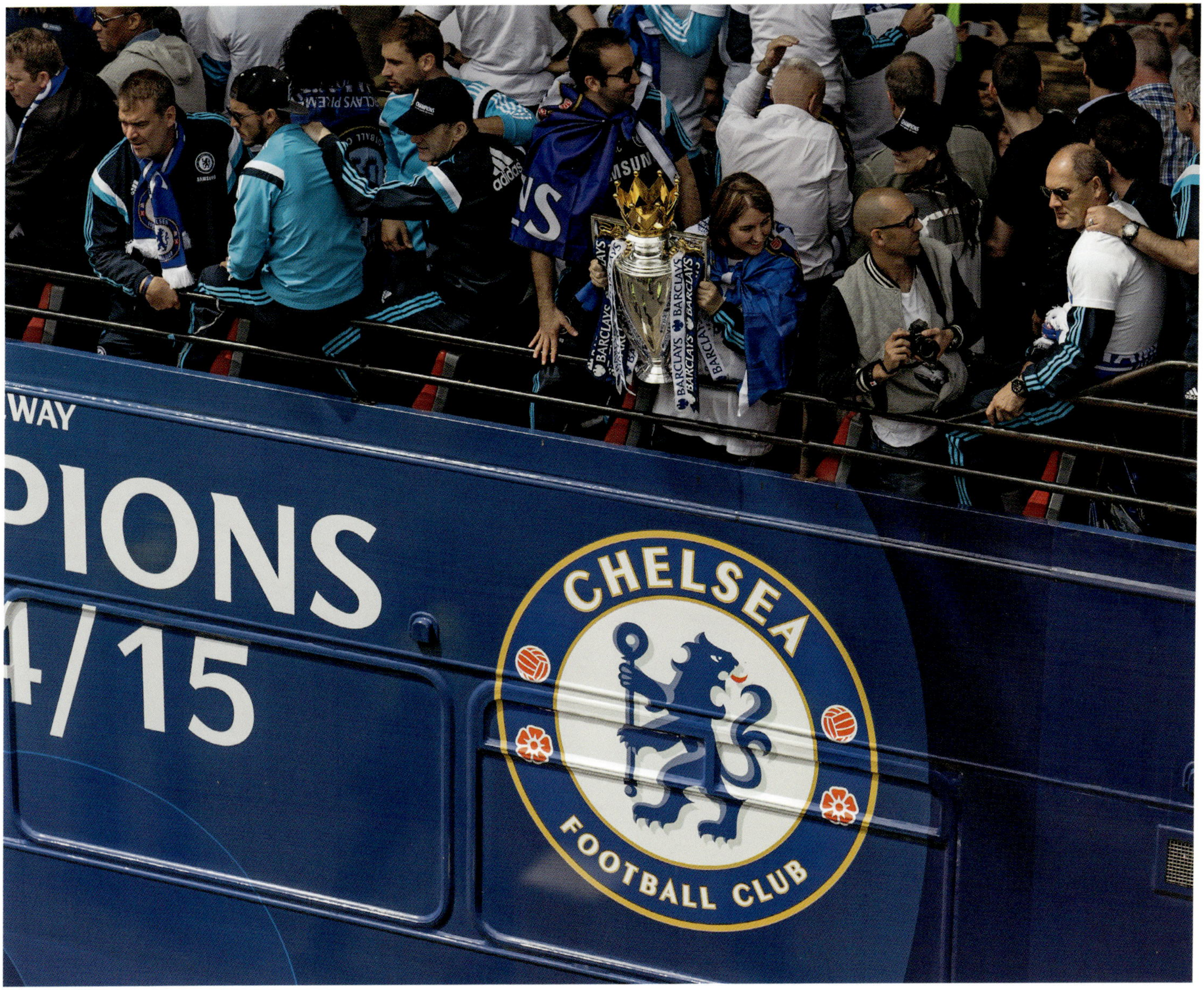
WAY
PIONS
4/15
CHELSEA
FOOTBALL CLUB

Surrey Classic & Prudential 100 Cycle Events

2015 saw the third running of this celebration of cycling. Since the success of the Olympic cycle event, the Mayor of London Boris Johnson, a keen cyclist himself, wanted to create a showpiece event using the Olympic route and harness some of that success. It takes place over the first weekend in August and on the Sunday Putney Bridge and the New King's Road are closed to cars so that everyone can enjoy the day. Unlike most of August it was a nice day. At the end of the day, whilst I was waiting for the elite group to come by, I was delighted to see this lady towing her children and her springer spaniel across the bridge.

Open Spaces

Two of Fulham's much loved and well used open spaces overlook the New King's Road. The larger, Eel Brook Common, which in 1554 was known as Helbroke meaning 'hill brook', was once a thirteen acre marshy common used by tenants for grazing cattle. Ditches were dug to alleviate the boggy problems and Charles Feret, the much respected local historian, wrote that in 1901 these were once well stocked with carp, tench, roach and even eels. The smaller Parsons Green was known in the 14th century as P'sonsgrene, the name deriving from the nearby parsonage to which the land belonged. In 1834 a cricket match took place between two teams of women, one of single and the other married ladies – the latter being the victors. For many years there was a large pond used by horses, dogs and ducks and, on occasions, for the immersion of converts by local baptists.

The church provided the land for two of the borough's public parks, the first being the 1891 Lillie Road Recreation Ground which had a splendid bandstand and gymnasium, since replaced by a leisure centre and other dedicated sporting facilities. Bishop's Park opened its gates two years later on a site adjacent to the moated Fulham Palace and locals flocked to enjoy the riverside gardens whilst children paddled in the lake and built castles on the sandy beach known as 'Margate Sands'.

The recently renovated smaller parks of Frank Banfield and Normand to the north of the borough together with the larger ones of South and Hurlingham in the south all provide up-to-date play areas for children, sports facilities for the more energetic and their well kept expanses of grass make perfect summer picnic venues. One of Fulham's hidden gems is William Parnell Park which lies near its eastern border with Chelsea and is locally known as Pineapple Park after one of its wooden sculptures. It also has a glow-in-the-dark path created by a spray-on coating which absorbs UV rays during the day, releasing them at night.

Despite the ever growing demand for more houses in London, it is reassuring that new open spaces are being created. The most recent is tree lined Imperial Park overlooking the Thames at Sands End and part of the regeneration plan for this former industrial area. Its boating lake and children's play area are much enjoyed by the young whilst the sensory garden is an ever welcoming haven of calm to older visitors.

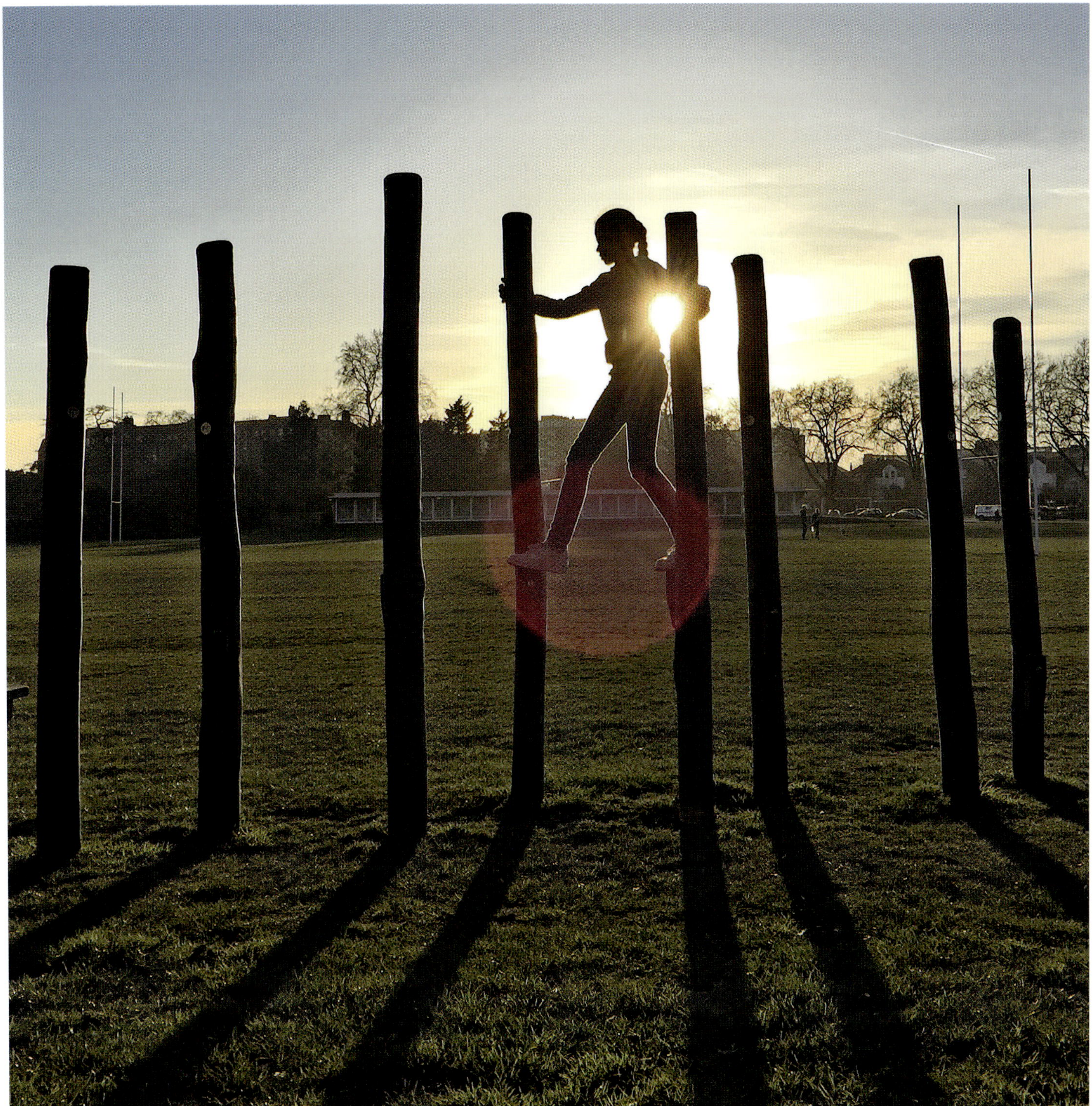

Fulham Palace

Fulham Palace was the Bishop of London's residence for over twelve centuries and served as a rural summer retreat for the Bishop and his family from the heat of the over-crowded and often unhealthy City. In the 20th century it became the Bishop's principle home until 1975 when it came under the jurisdiction of the local council. The medieval moat surrounding the Palace's former grounds stretched for 1.4km and was once the longest in England. Filled in during the 1920s, only a small part is still visible near the delightful pink cottage (top left) at the main entrance.

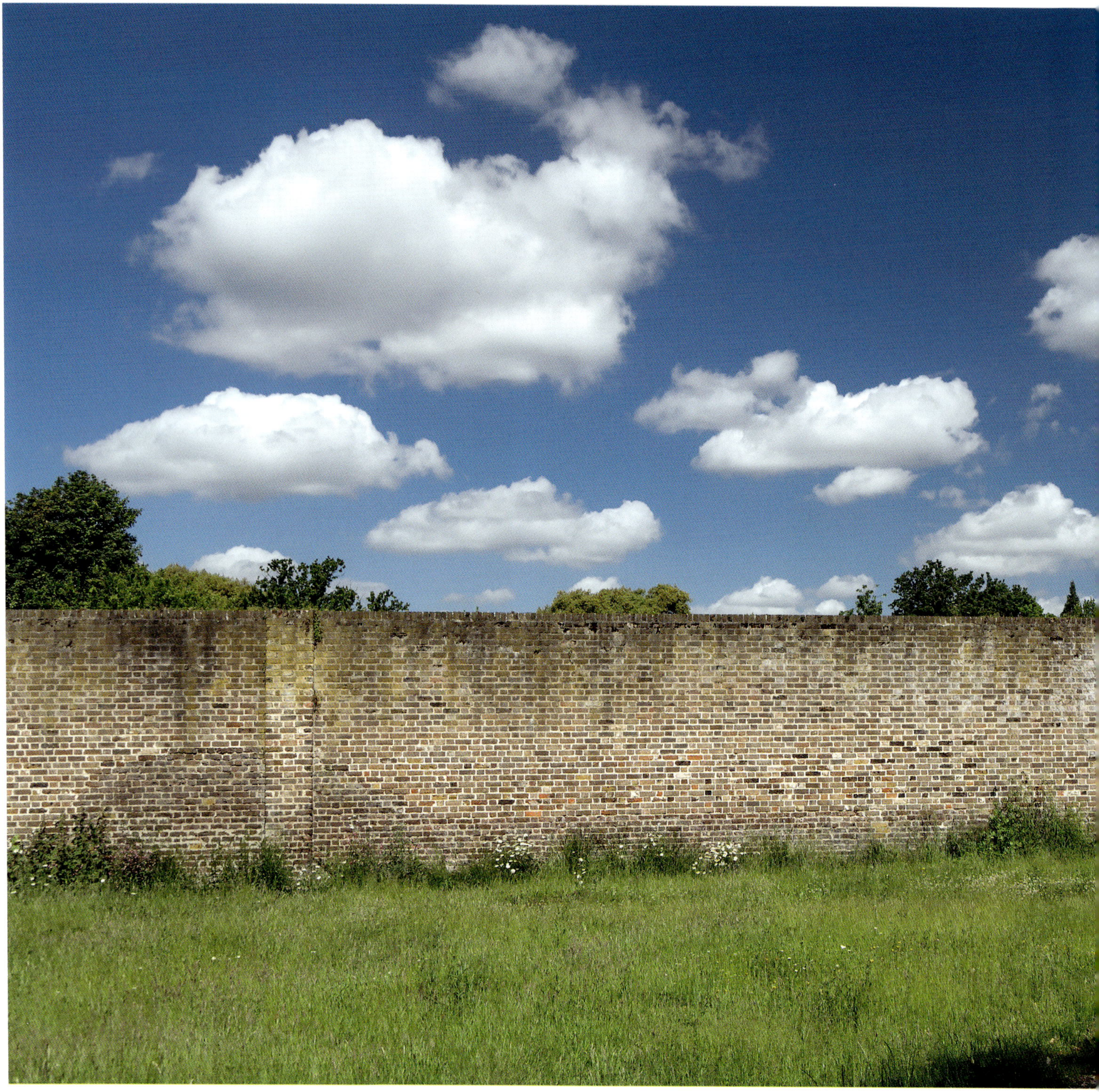

Within the borders of the Palace is a charming walled garden, which in recent years has undergone extensive restoration. The knot garden has been replanted to its original 1830's design and the shell of a vinery completely rebuilt. Garden paths have been laid out in their traditional position and new fruit trees planted.

Bottom right: I spied these diggings in October 2014 and never did discover what they were doing.

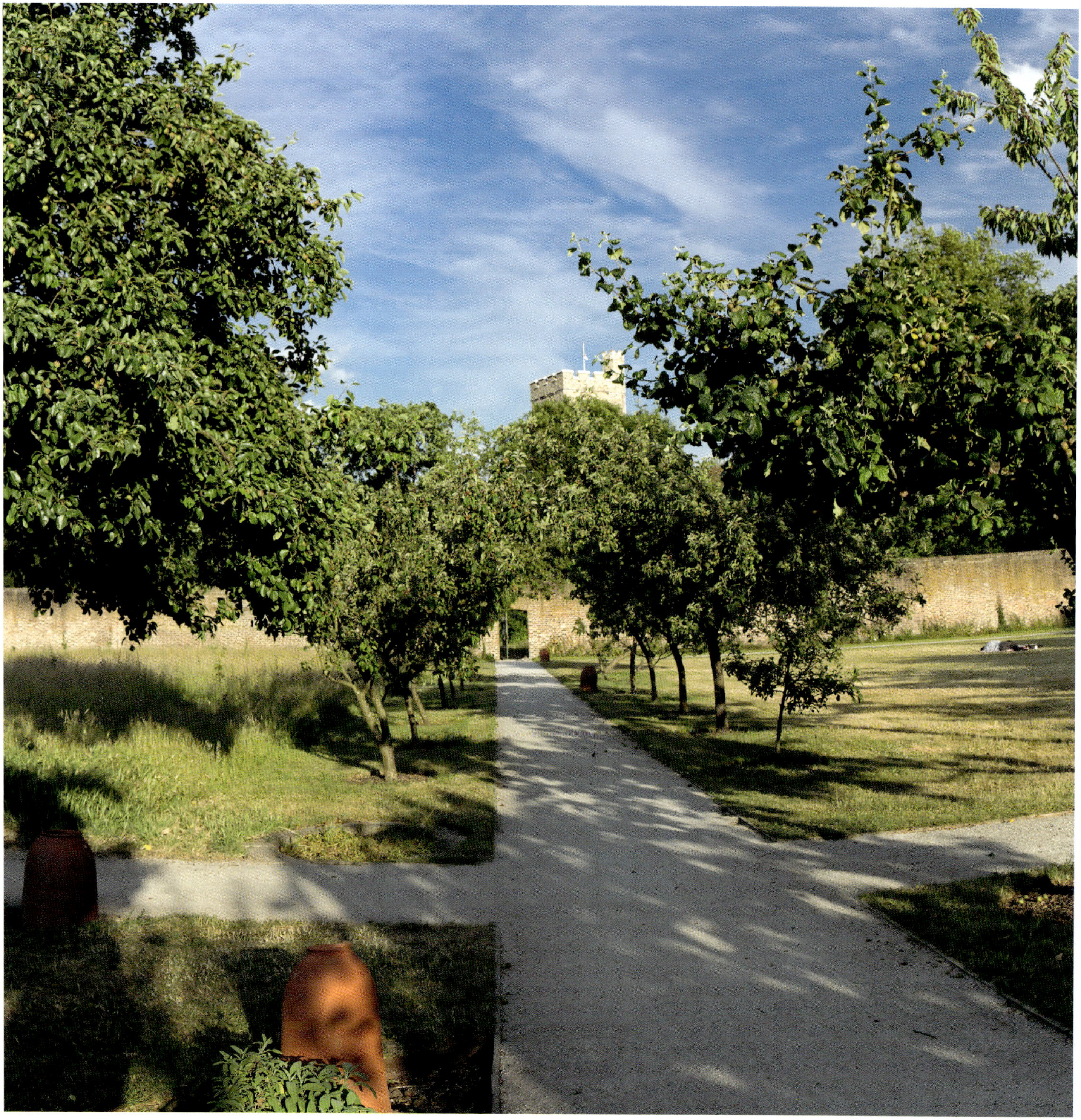

This spread: The Walled Garden through the seasons. You get an excellent view of All Saints Church from here, especially during the winter when there are no leaves on the trees.

Overleaf: Amongst the attractions of the Walled Garden is a large glasshouse. As a little bit of wild space in a busy metropolis the garden attracts many insects and even has a couple of bee hives. Top right: Red Admiral butterfly. Bottom left: Common Blue butterfly.

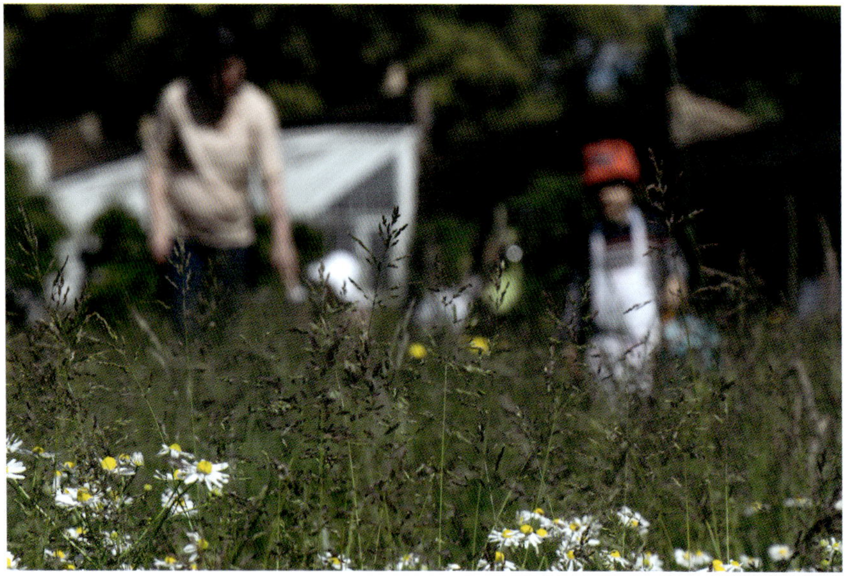

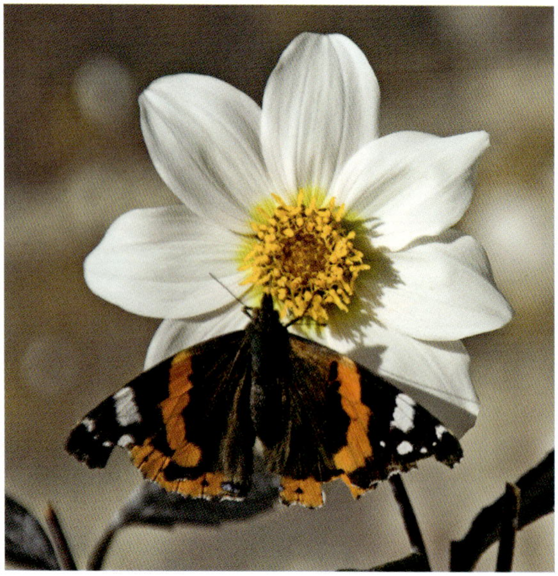

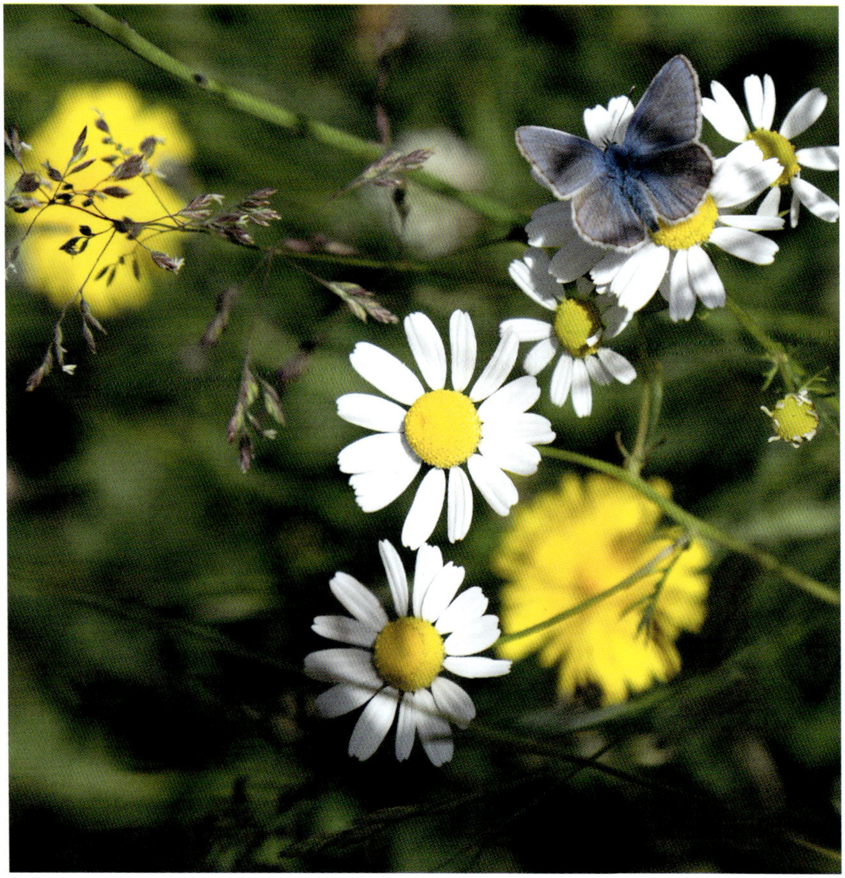

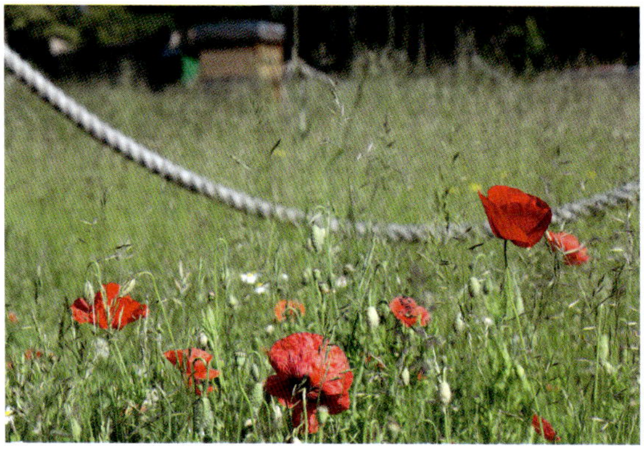

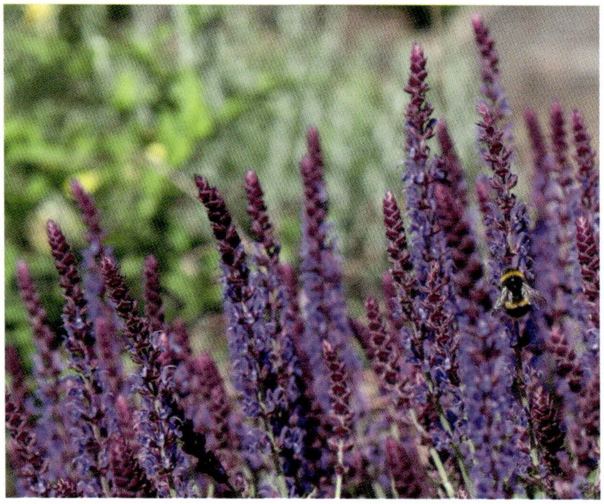

127

Fulham Palace Allotments

When I visited on their open day back in June 2015 I was interested to learn that the allotments were once an old Saxon burial ground. On account of this, plot holders are discouraged from digging too deep. Also, up until the '70s only men or widow's of plot holders could have plots. I am grateful to the ladies that I met for showing me around their plots – bottom left, from the left Nadia, Gill, Stef and Jill. Opposite bottom left, Bridget, who in true Saxon tradition, was in full costume as she displayed a wide variety of herbal remedies.

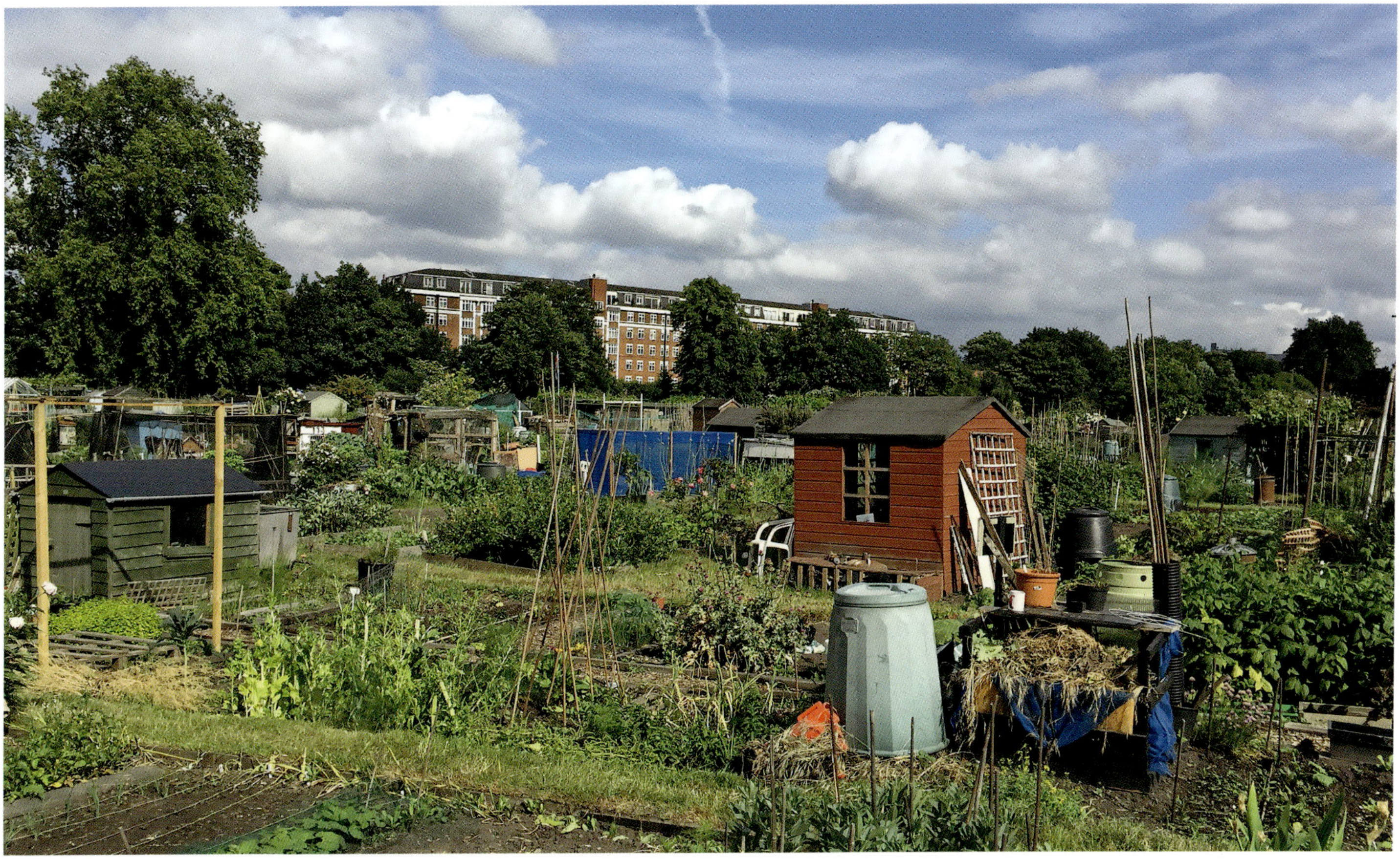

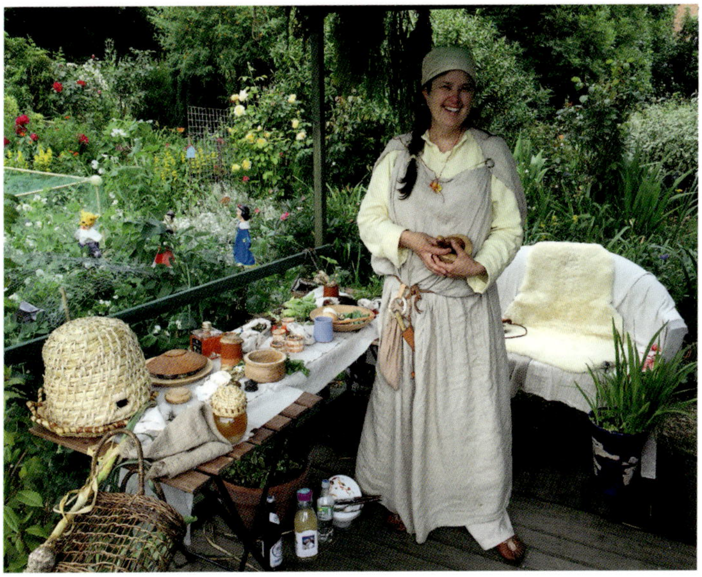

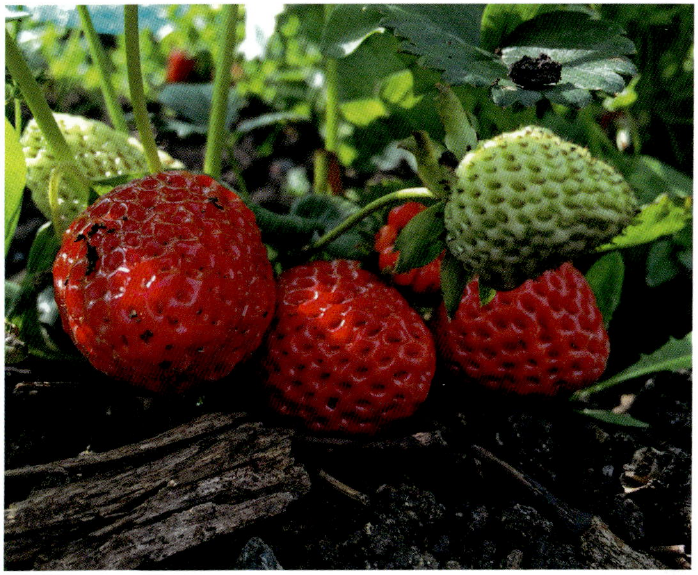

Hurlingham Park

Originally a polo ground for the Hurlingham Club, nine acres were acquired by the council in 1957 and became a multi-sports centre for Fulham's young and old alike.

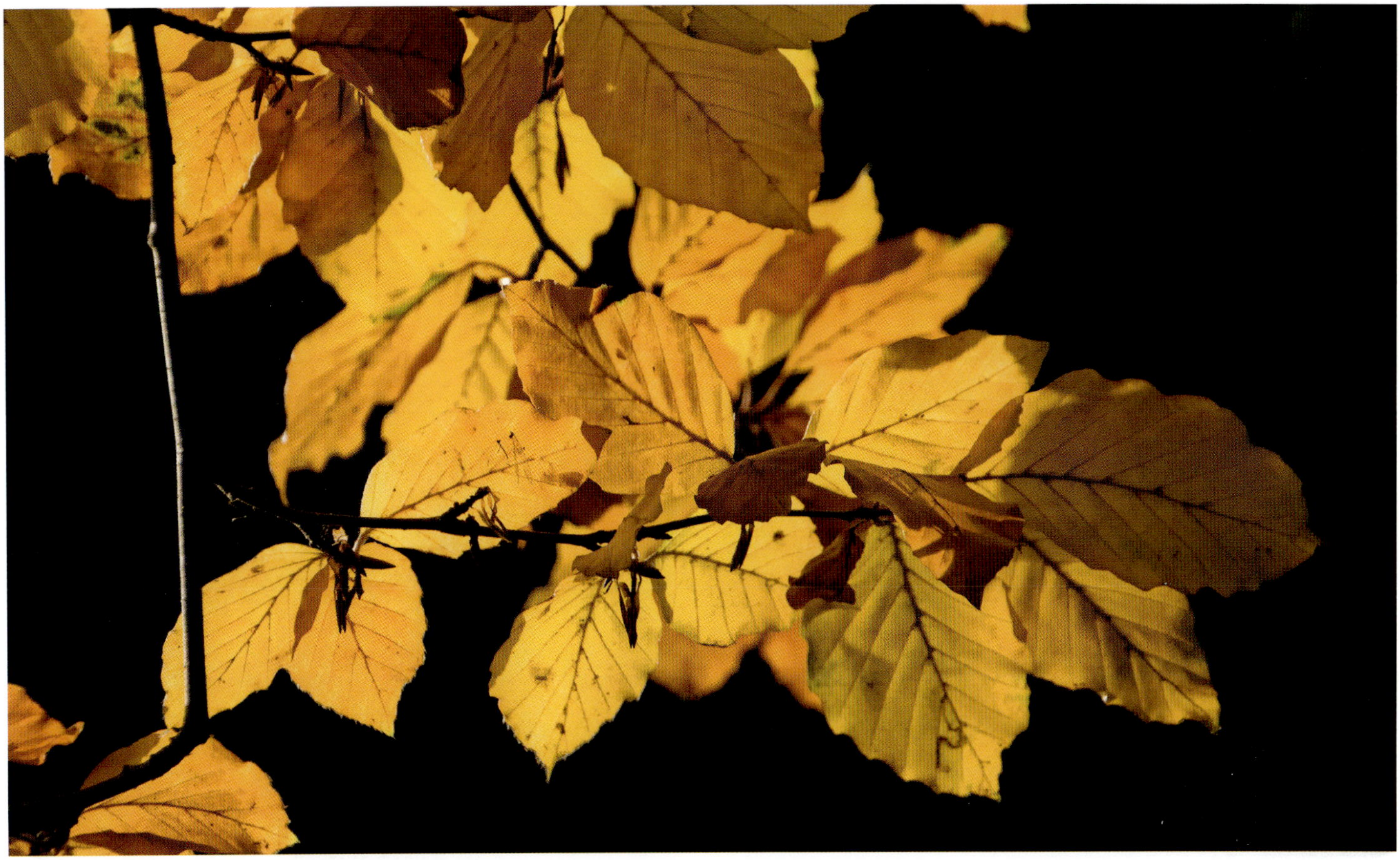

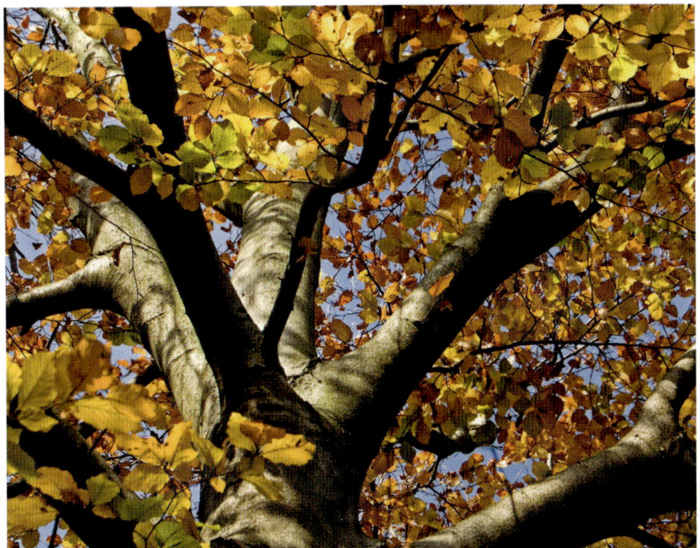

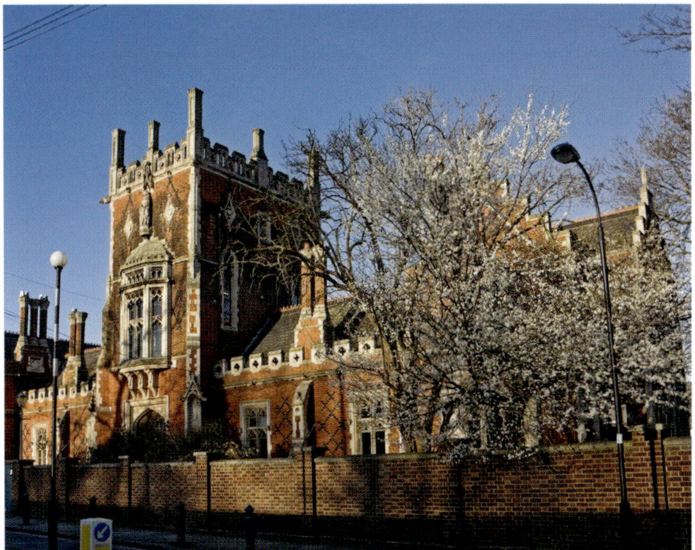

Hurlingham Park in the spring

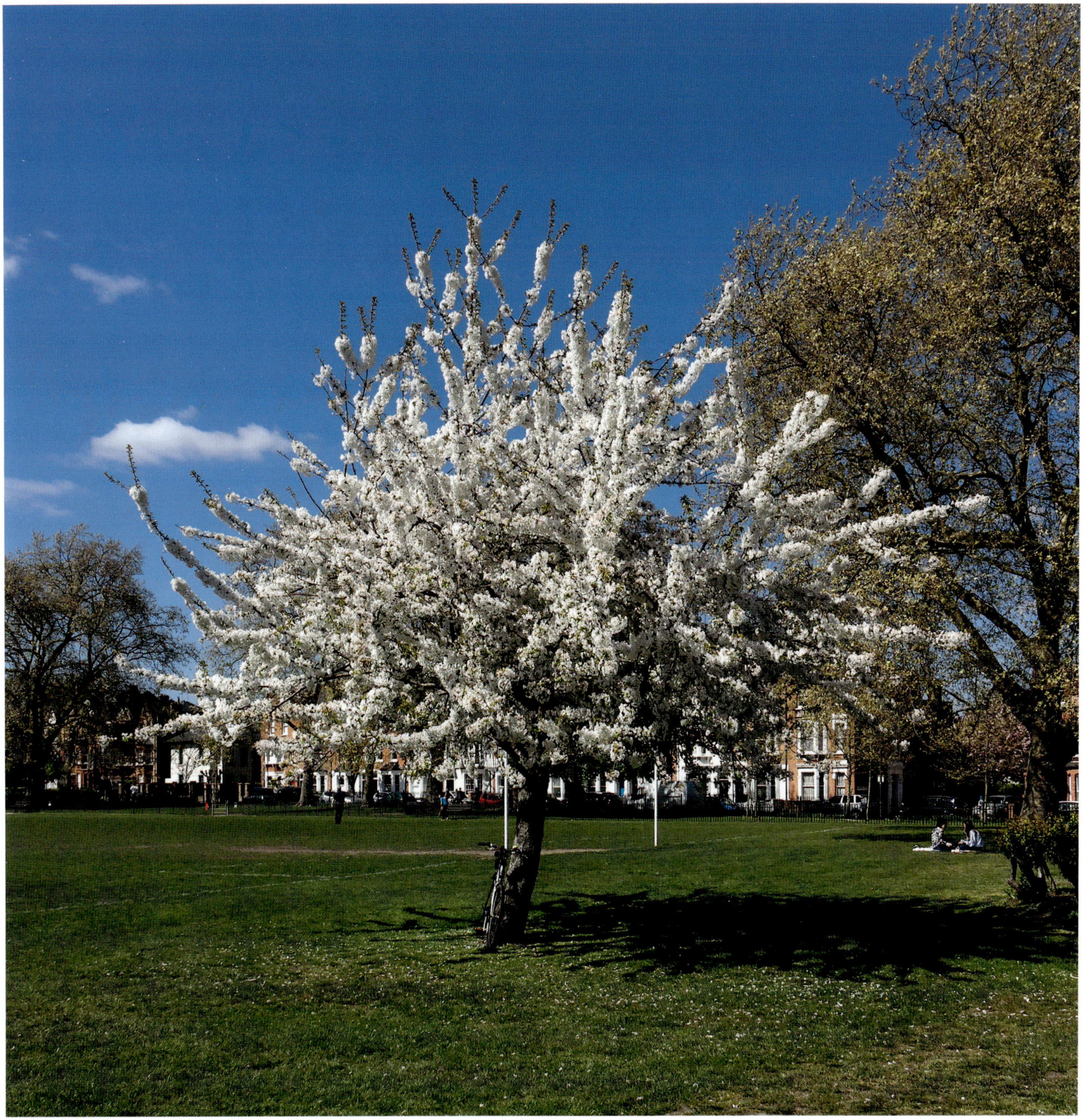

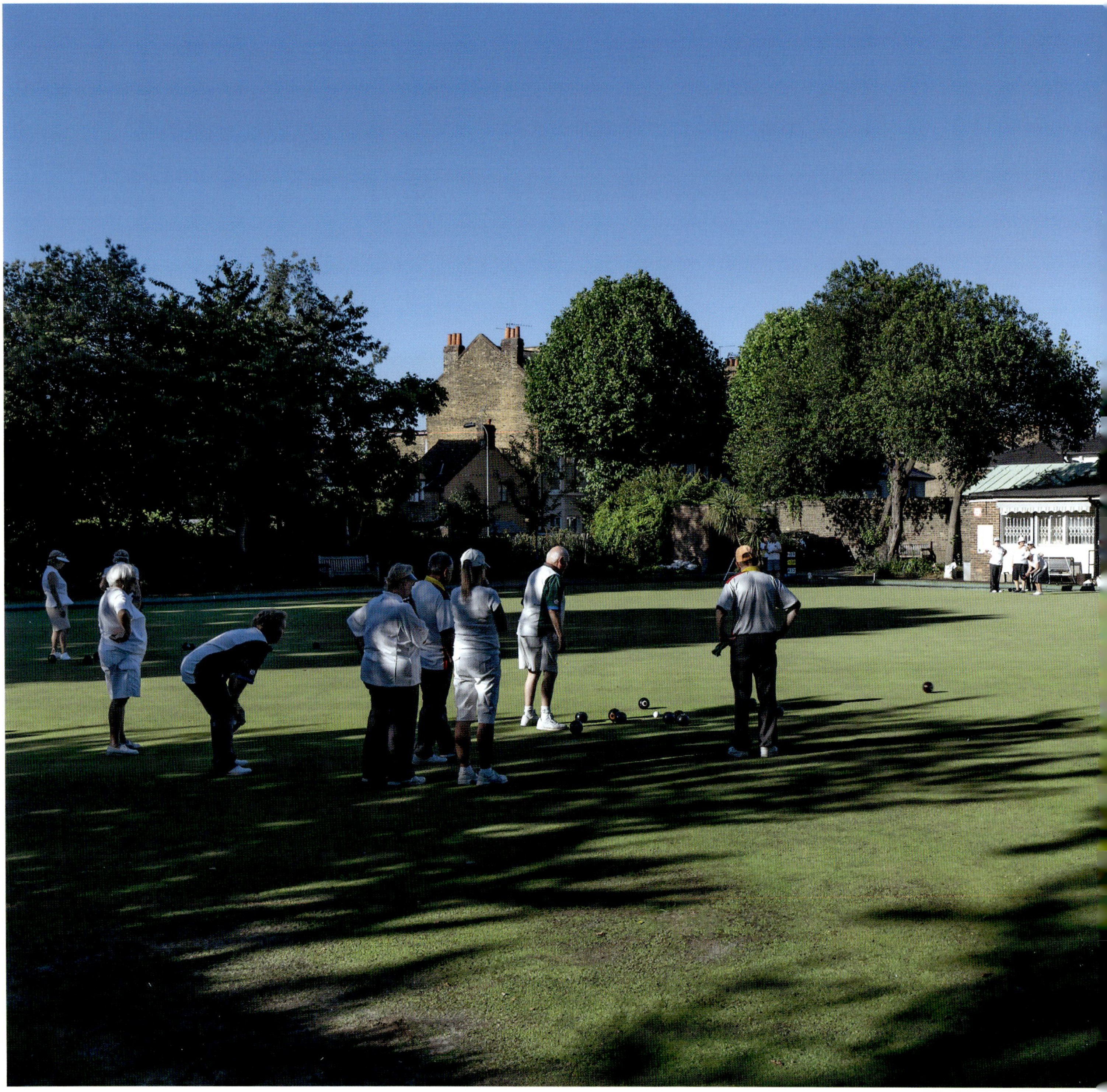

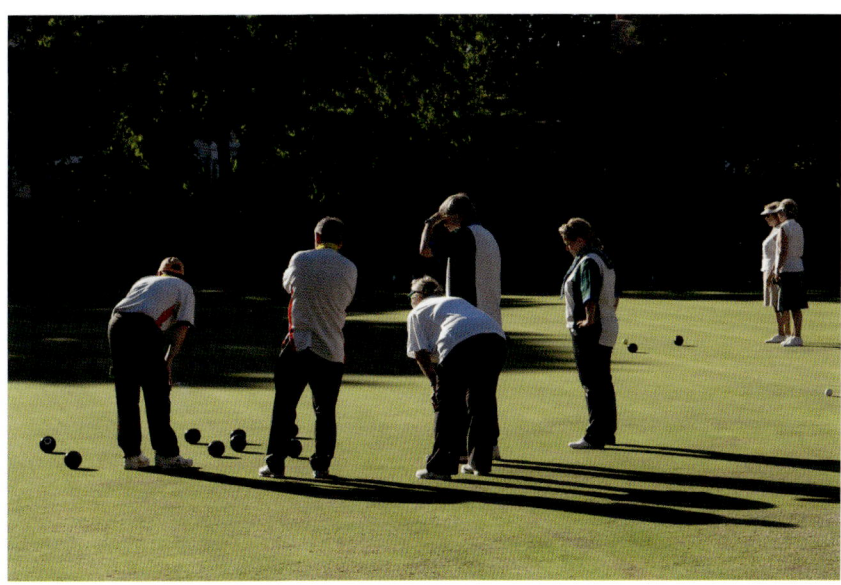

Tension mounts during a summer game of bowls at the Hurlingham Park Bowls Club. They are a friendly club and hold a club night on a Monday and new members are always welcome. Thank you to the club for letting me in to take these pictures. For more information please contact their secretary, Mrs Maureen Fairweather on 07908 106366.

Children take to the air in the new innovative wooden play area.

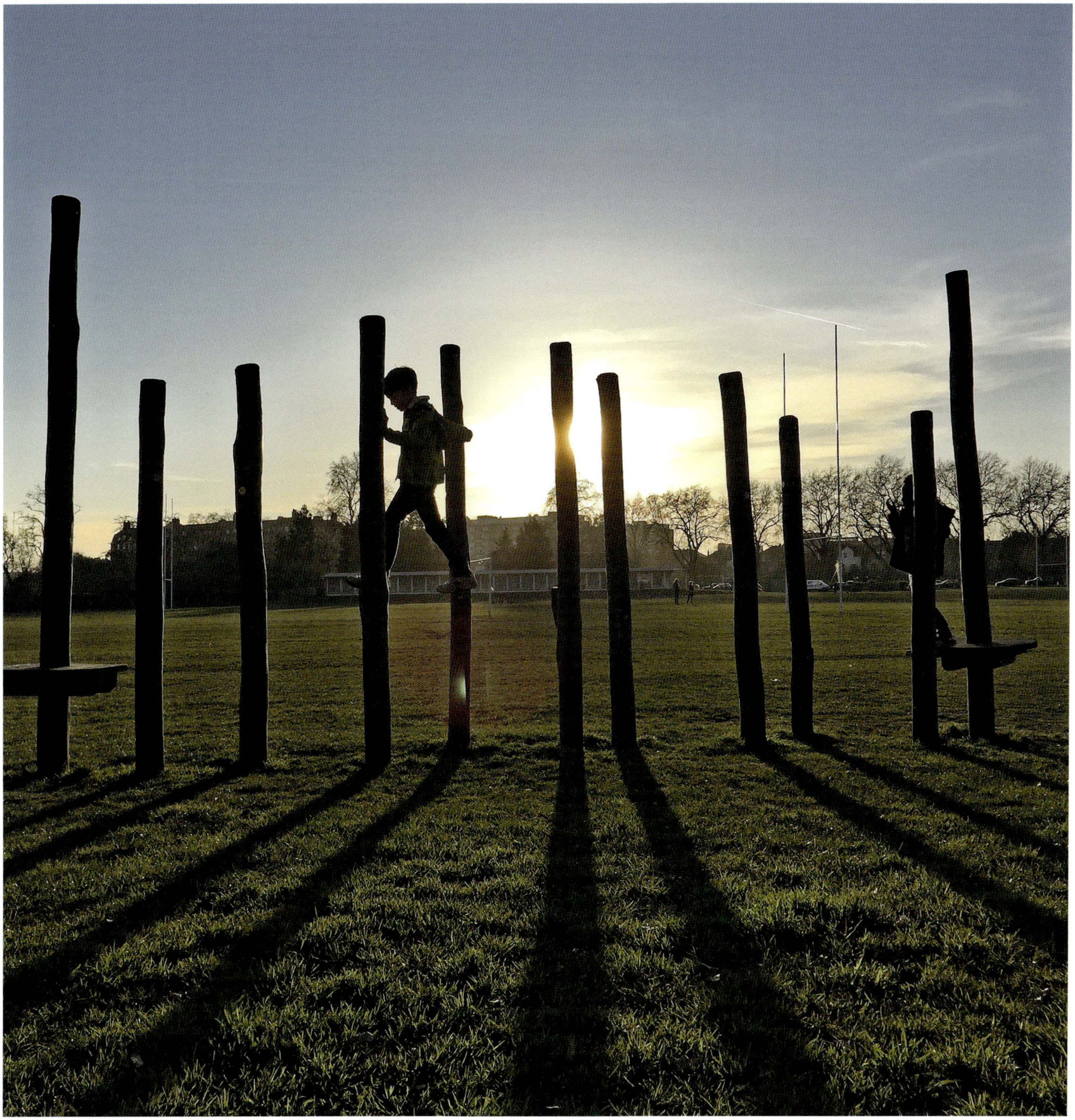

Polo at Hurlingham Park

Polo in the Park returned to Hurlingham in 2009 and each year the three day event brings the game back to its British roots. A new bore hole has been sunk in order to extract water and enable the park to remain green in the summer months.

Polo originated in Central Asia, probably Persia, and was popularised by the British during their time in India, the first polo club being formed in 1833.

The exclusive Hurlingham Club became the headquarters for polo in this country in 1874 and it remained here until the Second World War.

The Hurlingham Club

The club is centred on Hurlingham House, built in 1760 by Dr William Cadogan on a nine acre estate. Over the years wings were added to the central pillars neo-classical frontage and a further 16 acres of grounds were acquired.

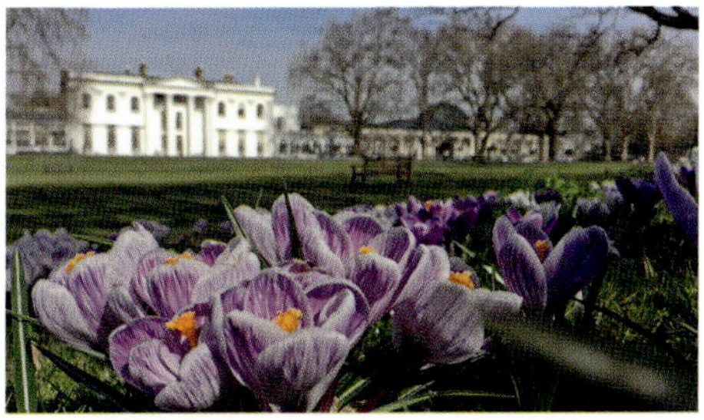
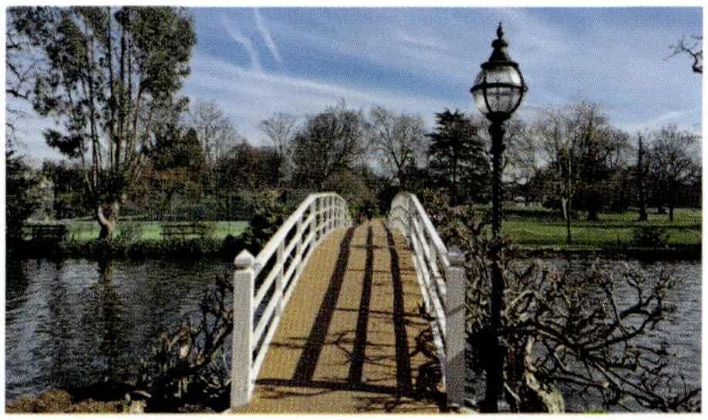
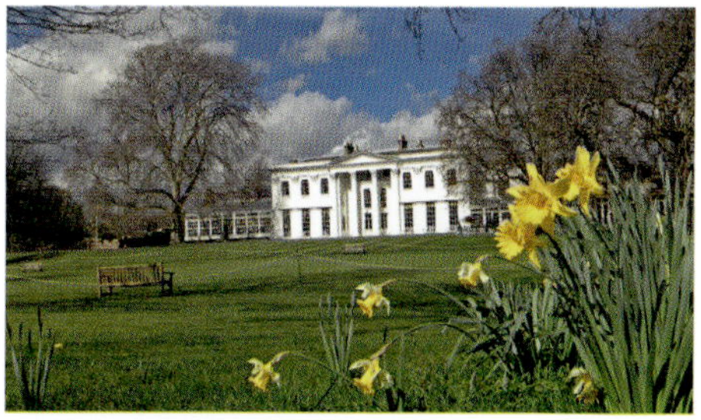
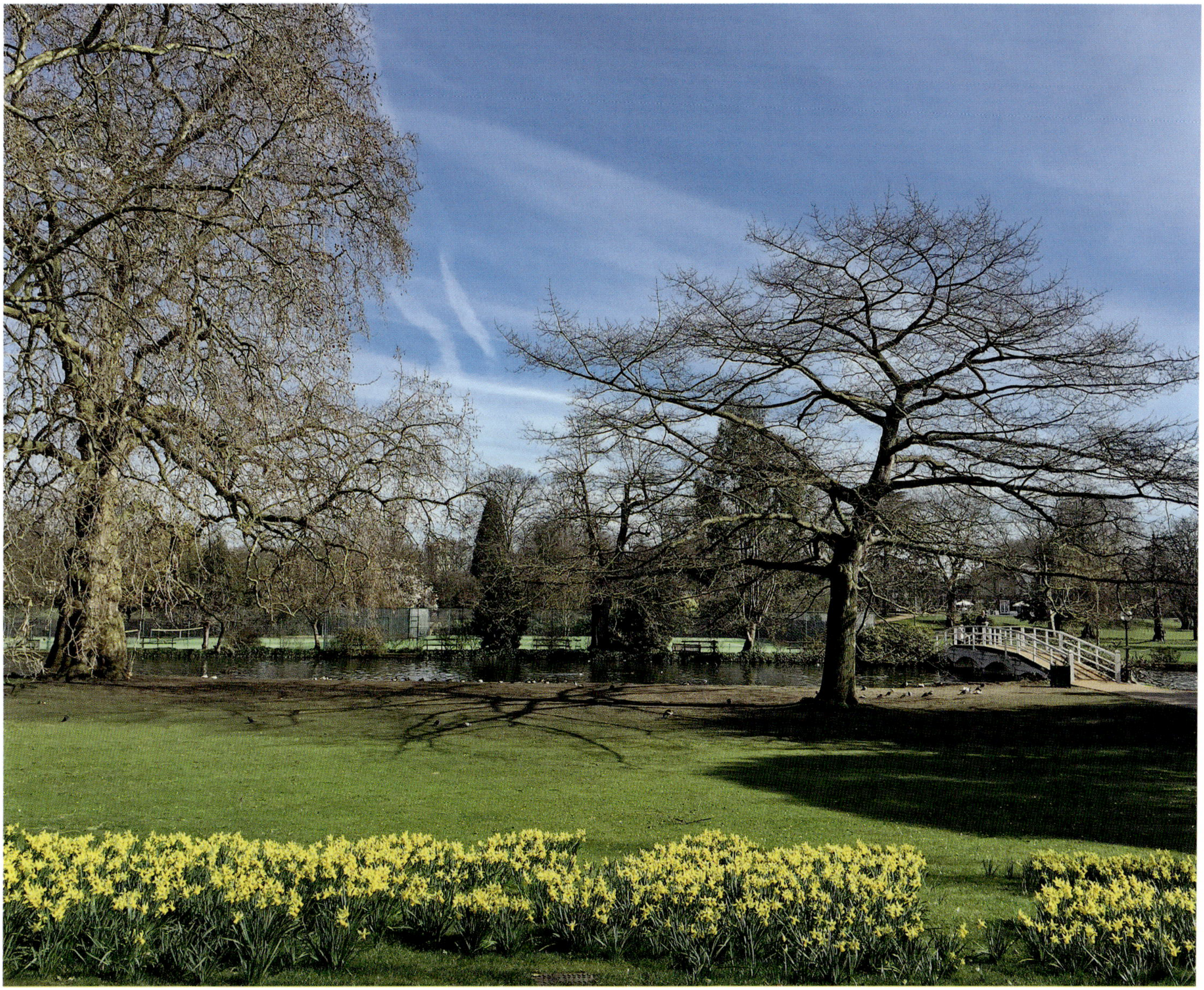

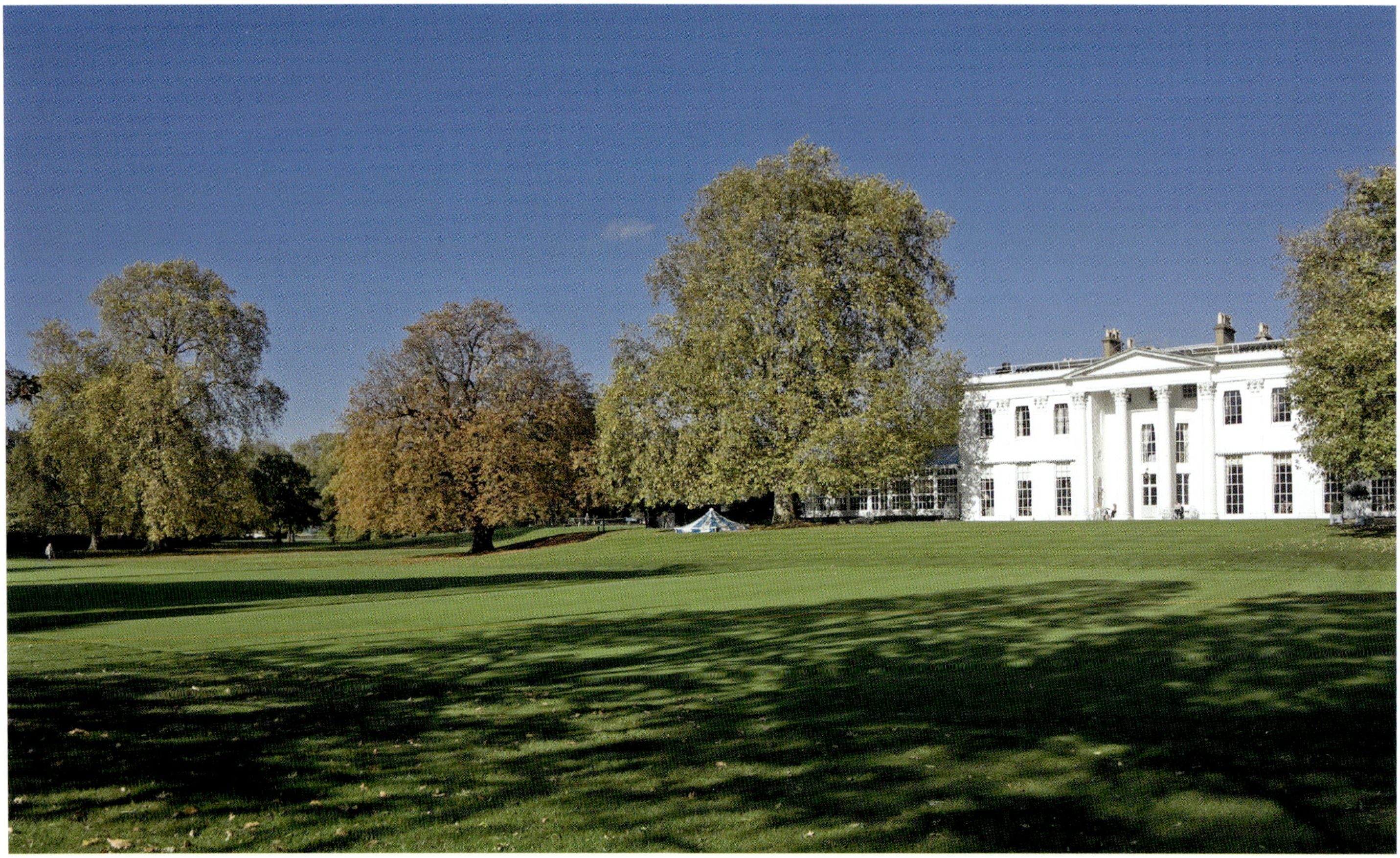

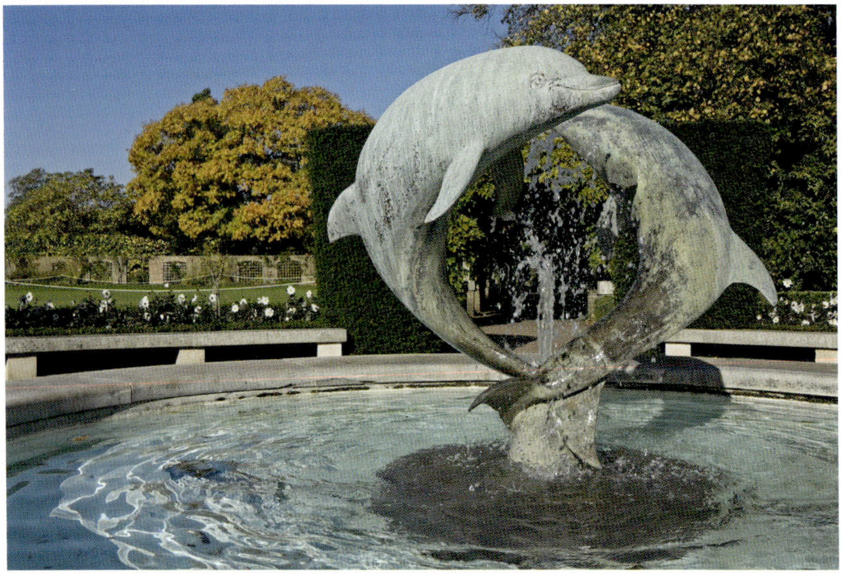

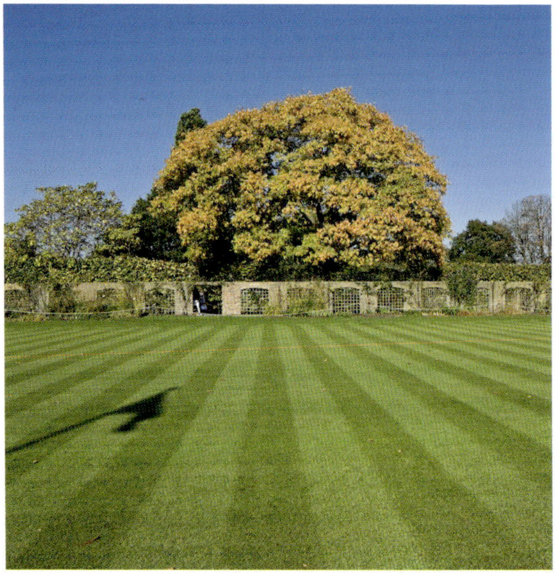

Around 500 AD a Saxon family called Hurla established a small ham, or farm, on the banks of the Thames which over the years became known as Hurlingham Fields.

In the Second World War an anti-aircraft battery and barrage unit was based at the club whilst the main polo ground was dug up for growing vegetables.

Opposite bottom left: The delightful sculpture of two dolphins by David Wynne was presented to the club in 1995 by the sculptor. Wynne sadly passed away in 2014.

South Park

South Park opened in 1904 thanks to local benefactress Miss Charlotte Sulivan who sold the land to the Fulham Borough Council with a covenant that it should always remain an open space.

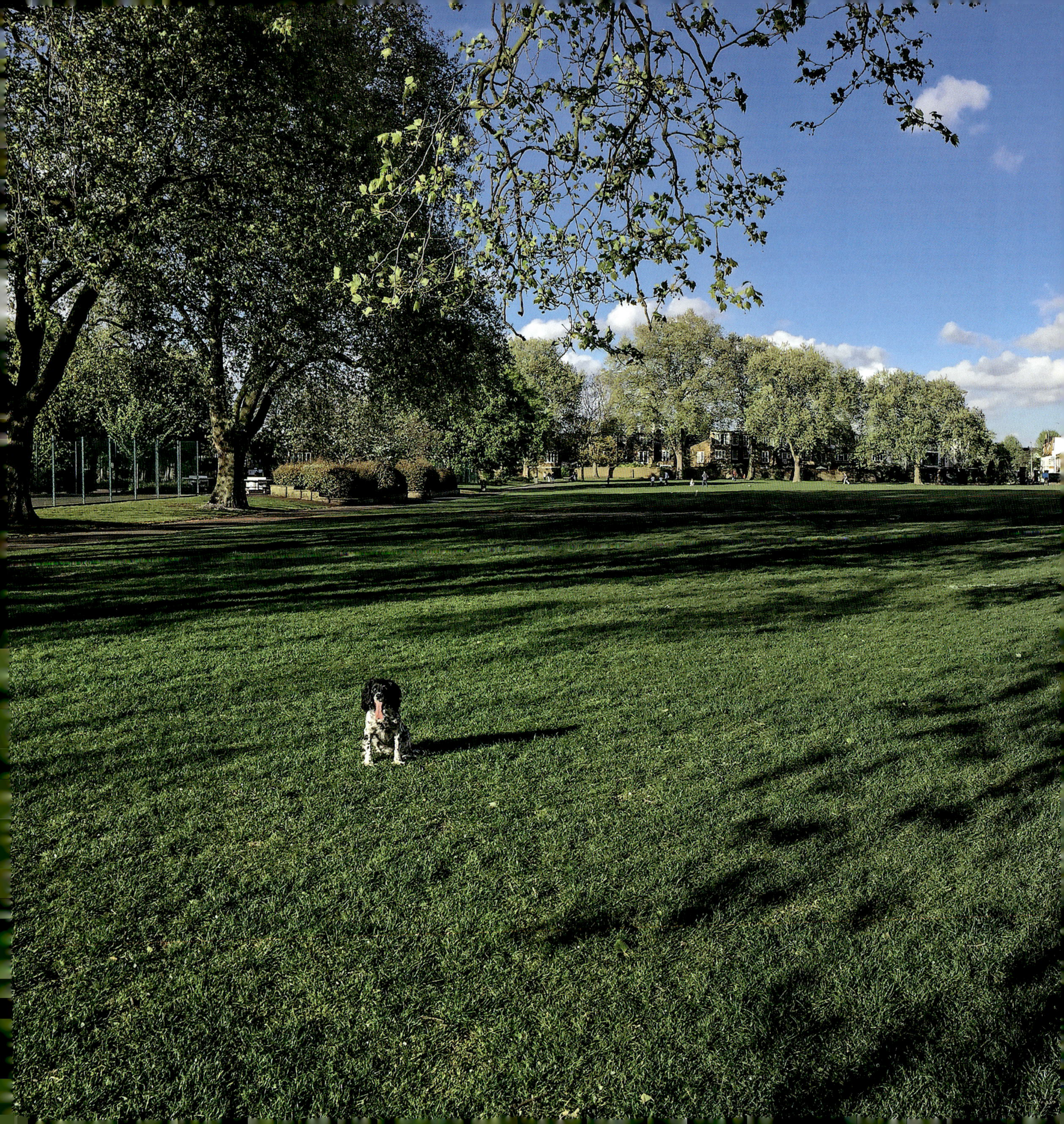

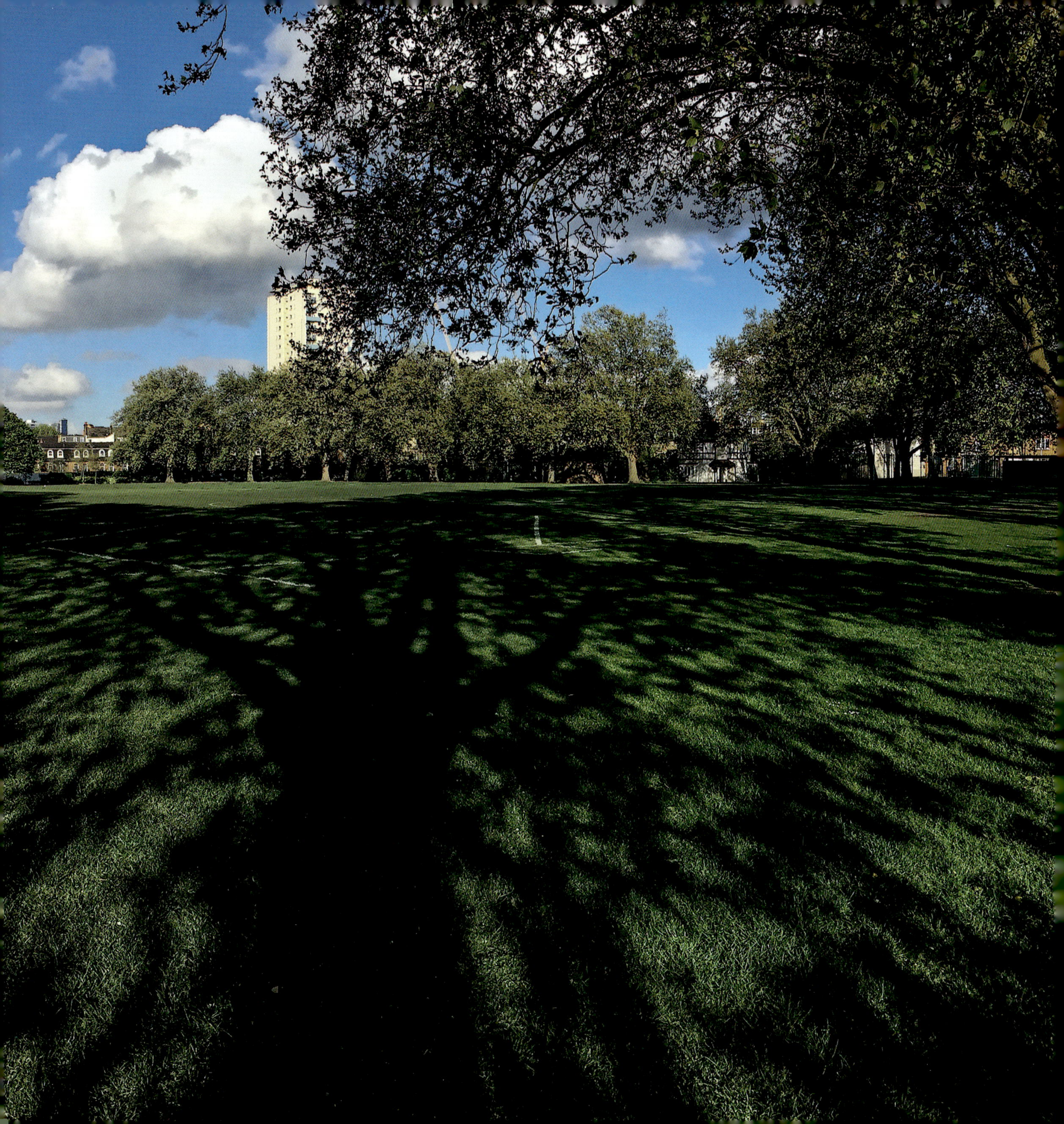

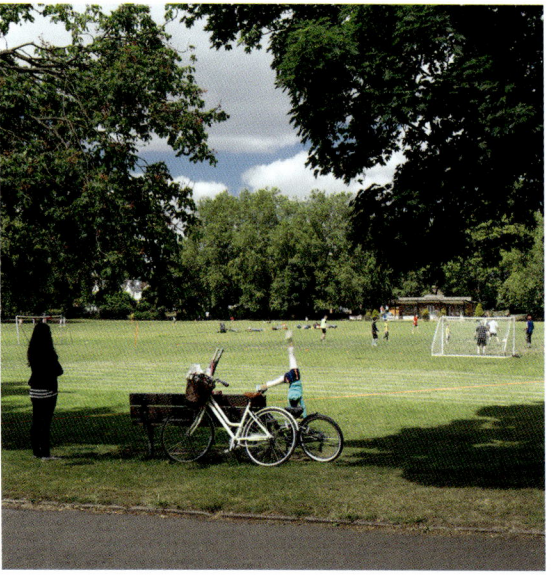

During World War II sand was dug from the park to fill sandbags needed to protect buildings in Fulham and air raid shelters were created near the present cricket pavilion.

151

The annual Picnic In The Park, organised by The Friends of South Park, is held in June. For more information on the park and how to join The Friends please visit www.friendsofsouthpark.co.uk

Popular attractions such as live music (left), fun fair rides (bottom left), and classic cars (below) like this police car.

When the park was opened the ceremony did not go as smoothly as planned as the crowds were unable to enter due to the gates sticking and the mayor was not able to wear his chain of office as the key of the Town Hall's strong room, where it was stored, had been mislaid.

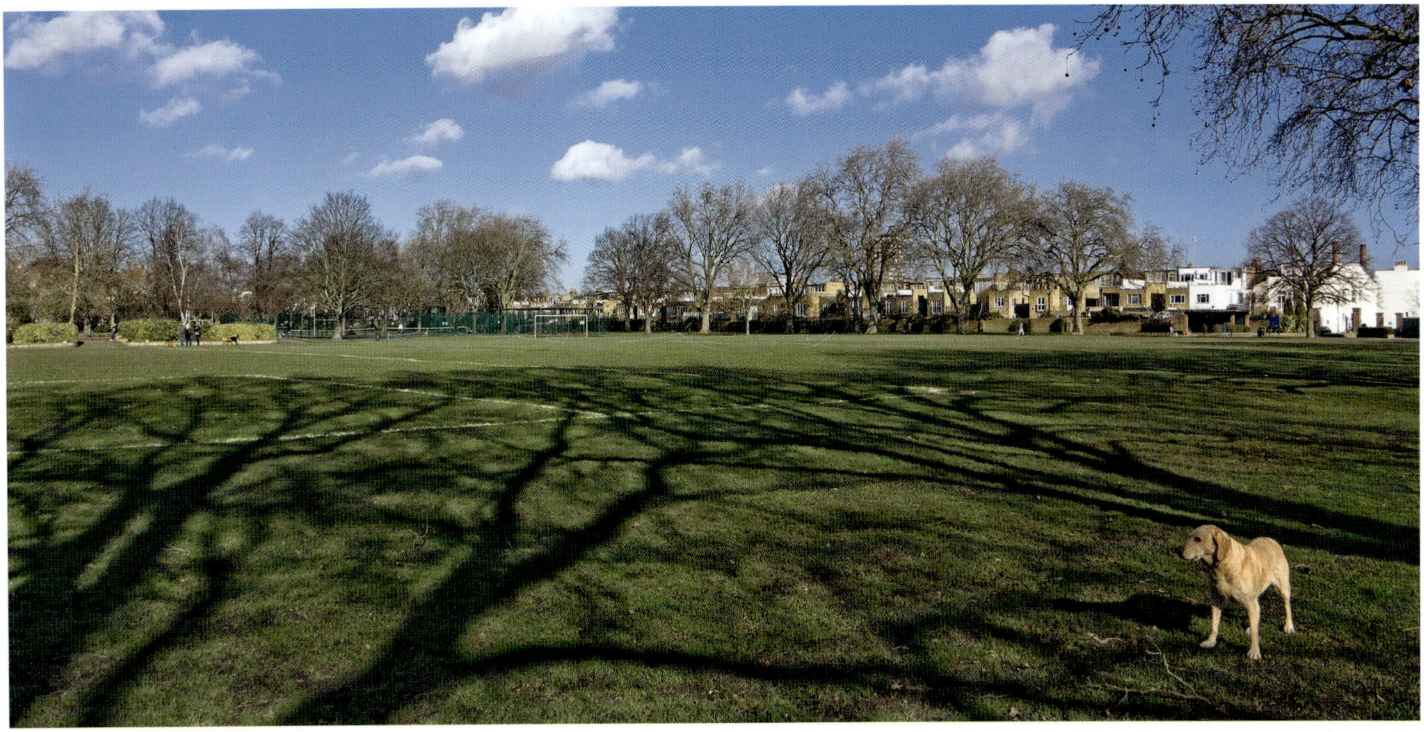

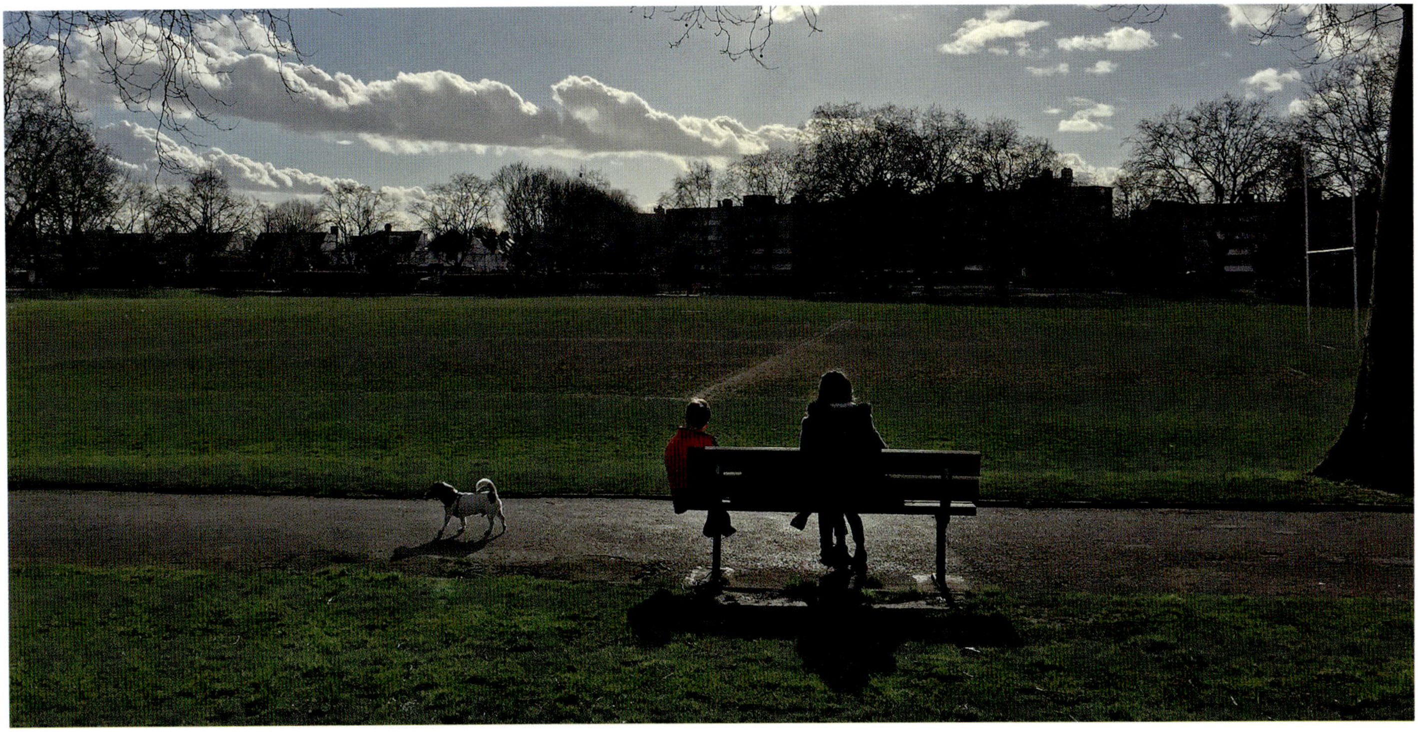

In the north west corner of the park, the Friends have a little garden given over to several allotments and some flower beds. As well as attracting lots of wildlife they also have a couple of bee hives. Nature notes from children at nearby Peterborough School at the turn of the 20th century record that a nightingale had been heard singing in the park.

156

157

Beside the park and just off Peterborough Road is Hurlingham and Chelsea School. The school is currently undergoing some renovation, with the new building (top left) replacing the previous one from 1956. Thank you to their business manager, Ian Ilett, for showing me around.

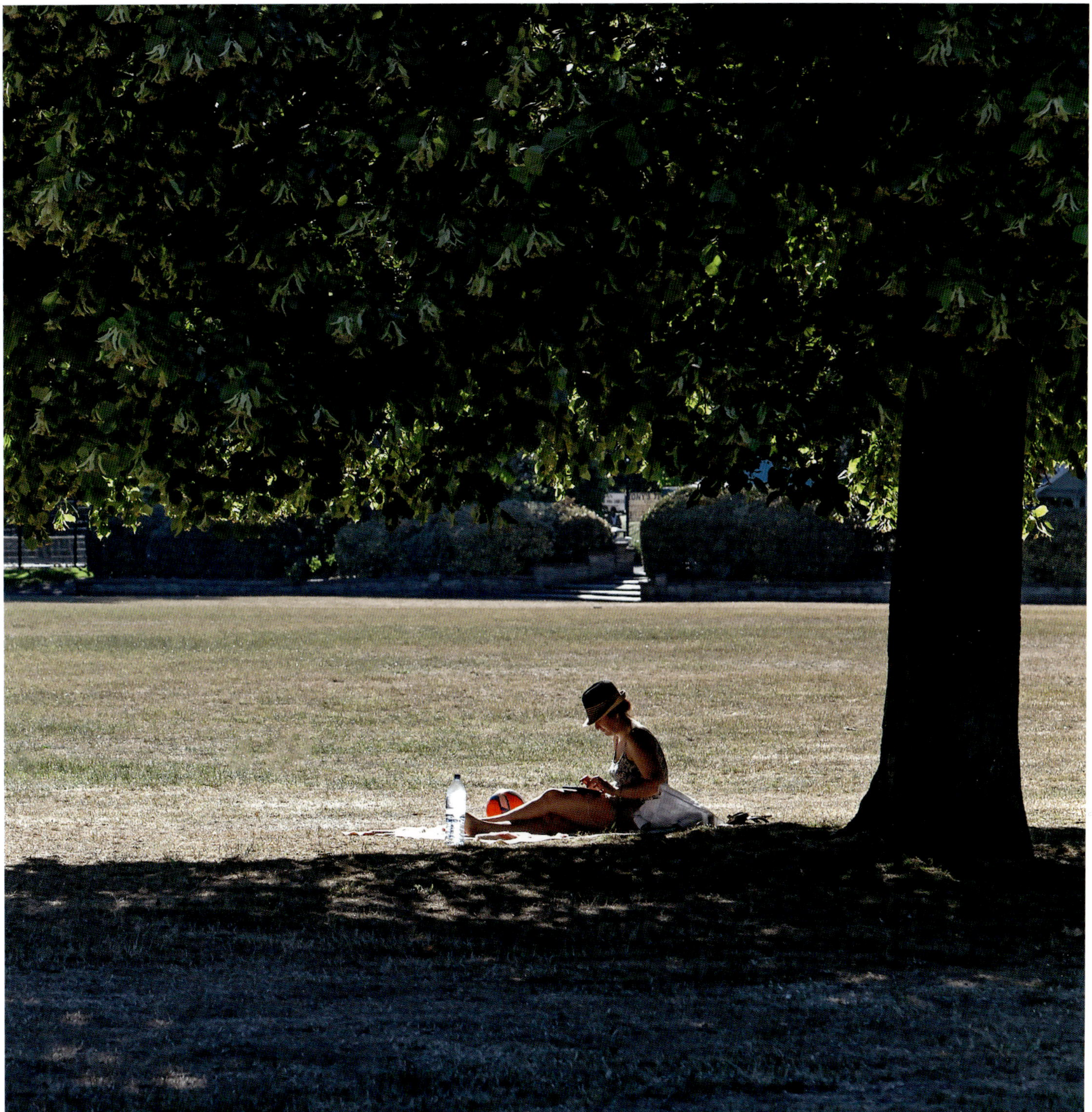

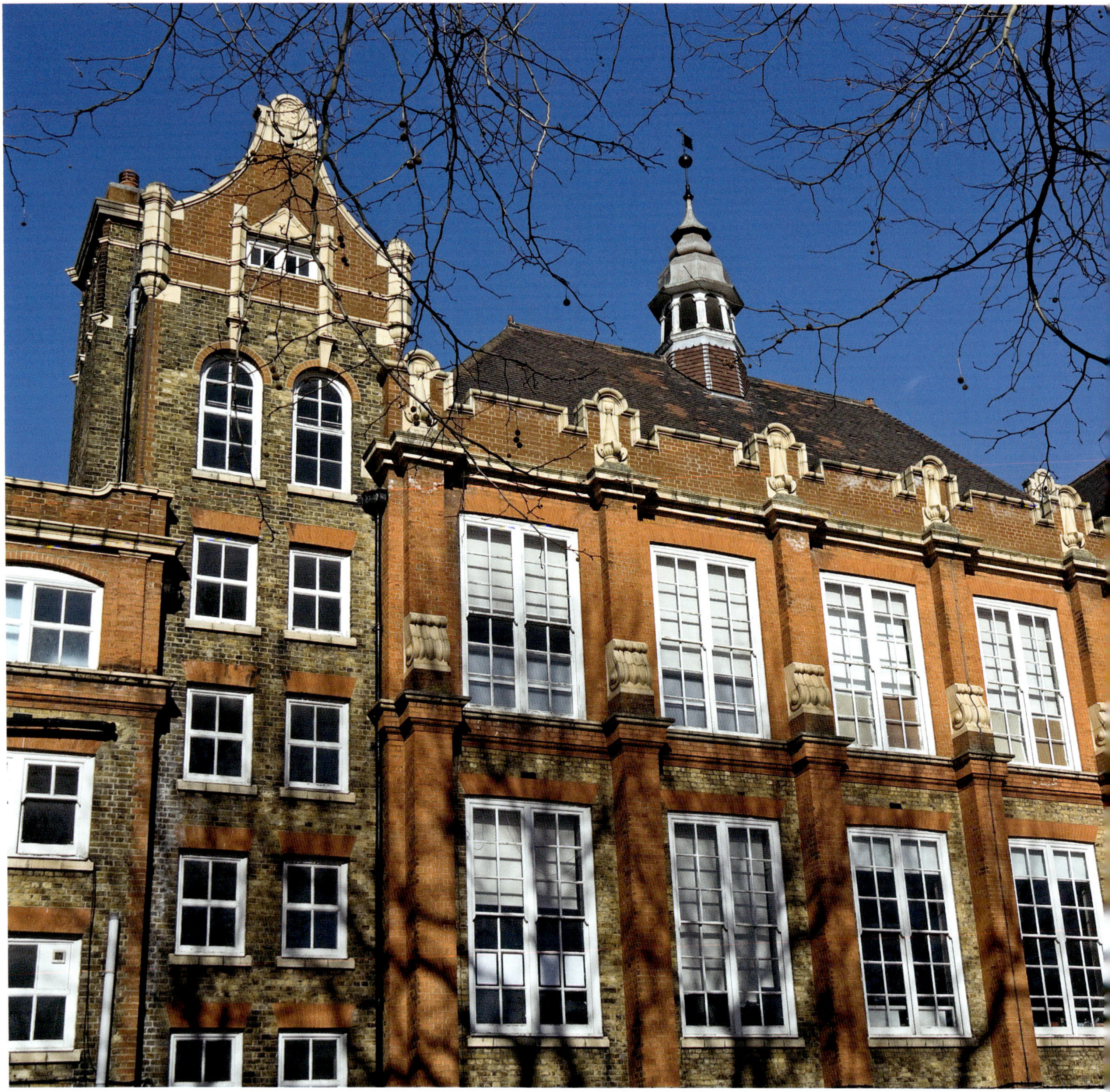

The schools built at the end of the 19th century overlooking South Park continue to educate local children in both English and French.

Bottom right: Thomas's Fulham preparatory school is located in a former Victorian school building.

The Queen's Club

The Queen's Club, which opened in 1886, was named after Queen Victoria its first patron. It is one of the premier lawn tennis and racquets clubs in the world.

The Queen's Club was the first multipurpose sports complex in the world. At first it hosted up to 25 sports, including football and rugby. These quickly out grew the ground's facilities and capacity and so moved to their own sites eg. Twickenham. Lawn Tennis increased in popularity and became the predominant sport played at the club.

Thank you to Anthony Wagstaff, their Communications and Membership Manager, for showing me around and also kindly setting up my visit to the Aegon Championships in June, (pictured overleaf). Firstly, the great Rafael Nadal just before he unfortunately exited the competition.

AEGON CHAMPIONSHIPS
BNP PARIBAS
The bank for a changing world
Retiready
AEGON
HIGHLAND SPRING
RADO
Europcar
Corona
ATP WORLD TOUR
LAN

165

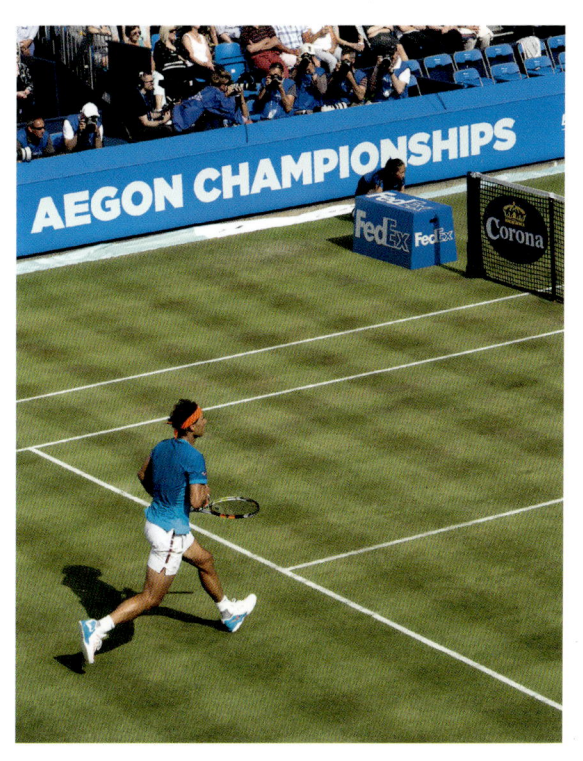

The prestigious annual Queen's Club Championships is one of the major competitions in the tennis calendar and is regularly voted by the players as their favourite tournament.

This spread: A victory by Andy Murray in the early stages of the competition. Murray went on to win the title in 2015.

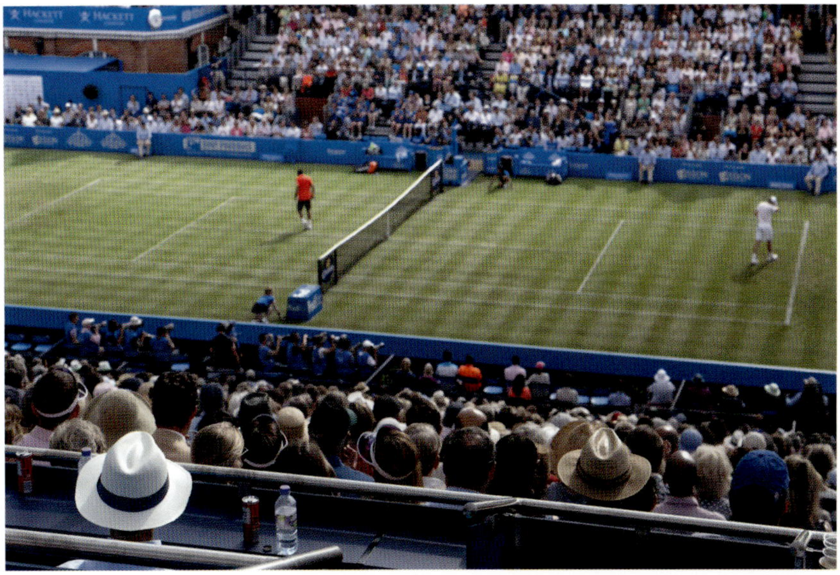

MOËT
MOËT & CHANDON
ICE IMPERIAL

HIGHLAND SPRING
LTA
BRITISH TENNIS

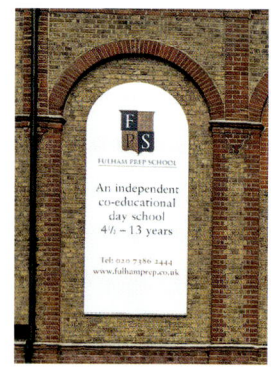

Opposite page: Fulham Prep School, in Greyhound Road near Queen's Club Gardens, is family-run and was founded in September 1996 by current principal, Mrs Jane Emmett. They have a junior feeder school on the Fulham Road on the approach to Putney Bridge. Thank you to Jane and her PA, Carolyn, for allowing me to take these pictures.

Left: William Gibbs, a local building developer, acquired twelve acres of wasteland adjacent to the recently opened Queen's Club and built an estate of mansion flats, each block named alphabetically after literary and historical figures. Described as 'classy' they were built to attract the more wealthy to Fulham – Arthur Ransome, author of 'Swallows and Amazons' was an early resident.

169

Eel Brook Common

Originally a village green, in 1832 horse races were held on the open space to celebrate the passing of the Reform Bill.

The artificial hard surface pitches were sponsored by Chelsea Football Club. Residents complained about the bright blue colour of the turf so a fence was erected around the pitches to prevent further annoyance.

Fulham Football Club played its first game on the Common in 1883, before moving to their permanent home at Craven Cottage.

173

William Morris, one of the most significant figures in the Arts & Crafts Movement and founder of the Hammersmith Socialist League often addressed large crowds on Eel Brook Common in an attempt to win new members for the party.

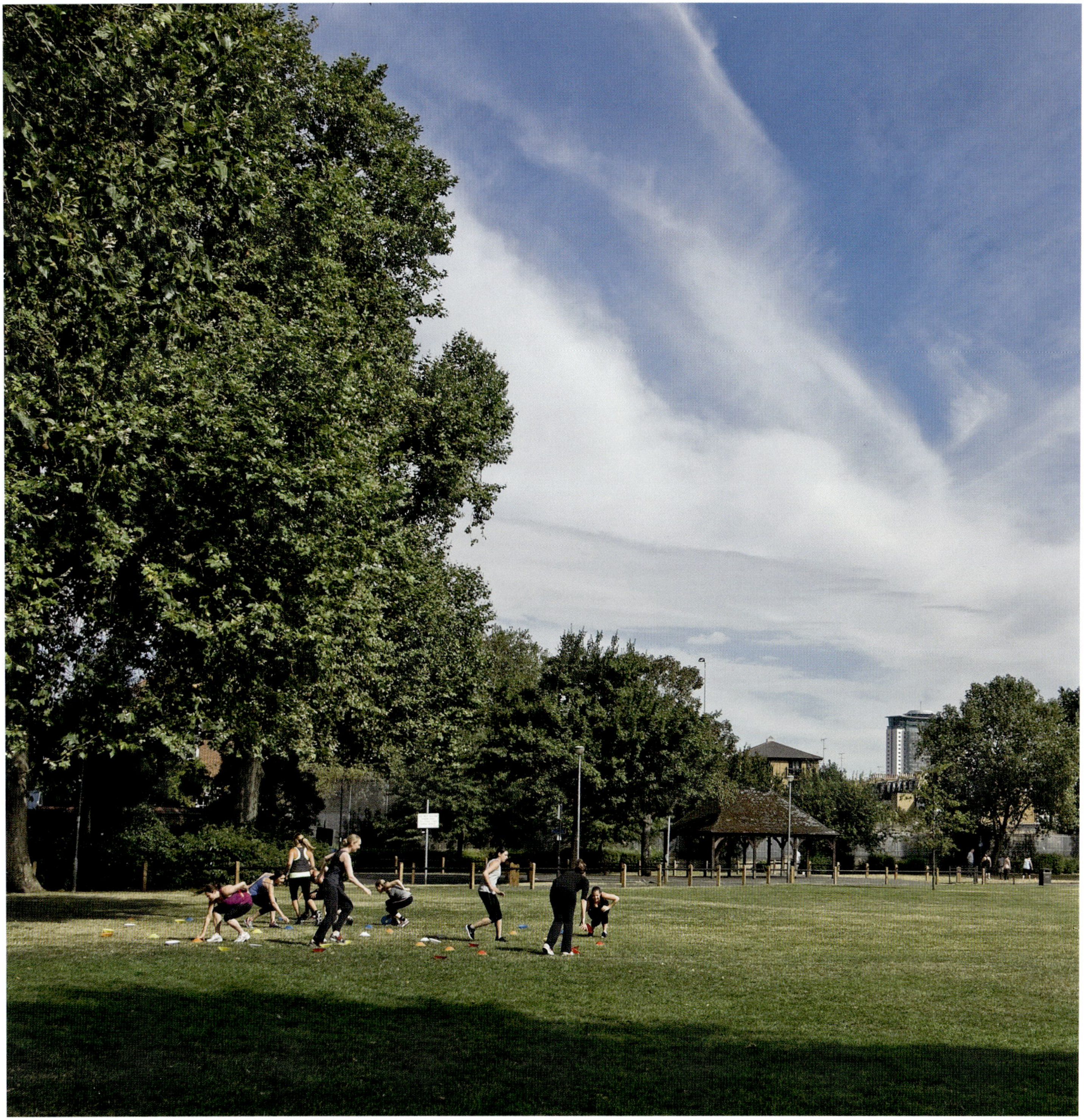

Fulham Cemetery

Opening in 1865, Fulham Cemetery was designed with an entrance lodge, two chapels and laid out with a grid of walks. Its grassy acres with leaning Victorian grave stones provides a peaceful haven and has a wonderful display of blossom in the spring.

178

Right: The First World War grave of Private Samuel Eric Freeman, a soldier in the Machine Gun Corps who died, aged 24, on 28th October 1918.

Normand Park

In the 1650s an imposing house was built on Norman's Land by Thomas Wyld. Normand House, as it came to be known, remained in the family for over a hundred years but by the 19th century it was an insane asylum for young ladies, subsequently a school and finally home to nuns of the Order of St. Katherine. After receiving a direct hit in the last war, the site was cleared and Normand Park laid out.

181

The Riverside

The riverside has attracted many splendid houses over the centuries, the first being Fulham Palace, the Tudor country home of the Bishops of London and during the 18th century it was joined by Hurlingham House which remains as a private club with gardens stretching to the river. The Ranelagh estate has long gone but the name lives on in local streets and residential buildings. Sands End stretches from the Creek which divides Fulham from Chelsea to Wandsworth Bridge Road and it was here that the Imperial Gas and Light & Coke Company established their works in 1824 followed by tile manufacturers, biscuit factories and laundries. Wharves were built for barges and boats to load and unload but as the gas works and factories moved elsewhere so these too have now all but disappeared. Soaring apartment blocks stand on former Imperial Wharf and south of Hammersmith bridge at Fulham Reach the site of Manbre & Garton's sugar factory has been replaced with glass fronted offices. The farm at Crabtree has also disappeared and Fulham football supporters fill the riverside garden of the pub which carries its name after cheering on their team at the nearby stadium which stands on the site of the long gone charming thatched Craven Cottage.

Whilst winters have not been cold enough to allow a Frost Fair to take place on the river's frozen surface since the 1790s, it continues to be a source of enjoyment for many. Tourists on pleasure boats travelling from Westminster Pier to Hampton Court and back are sailing on the same route enjoyed by the Sharp family whose music parties on their yacht are immortalized by the 18th century artist Johan Zoffany. The crews from numerous boat houses across the way in Putney are out in force each weekend and the blue and white sails of the South Bank Sailing Club's boats are a colourful addition to the water whilst on a spring day thousands crowd the banks to cheer the eights from Oxford and Cambridge universities as they row their hearts out in the annual Boat Race from Putney to Mortlake.

There is certainly nothing more delightful on a sunny day to walk through Bishop's Park as the sun sparkles on the softly flowing water, watch a heron patiently waiting in the shallows and a cormorant dive and then emerge triumphant with a fish in its beak, something residents of Fulham have enjoyed over the centuries and will continue to do so for many years to come.

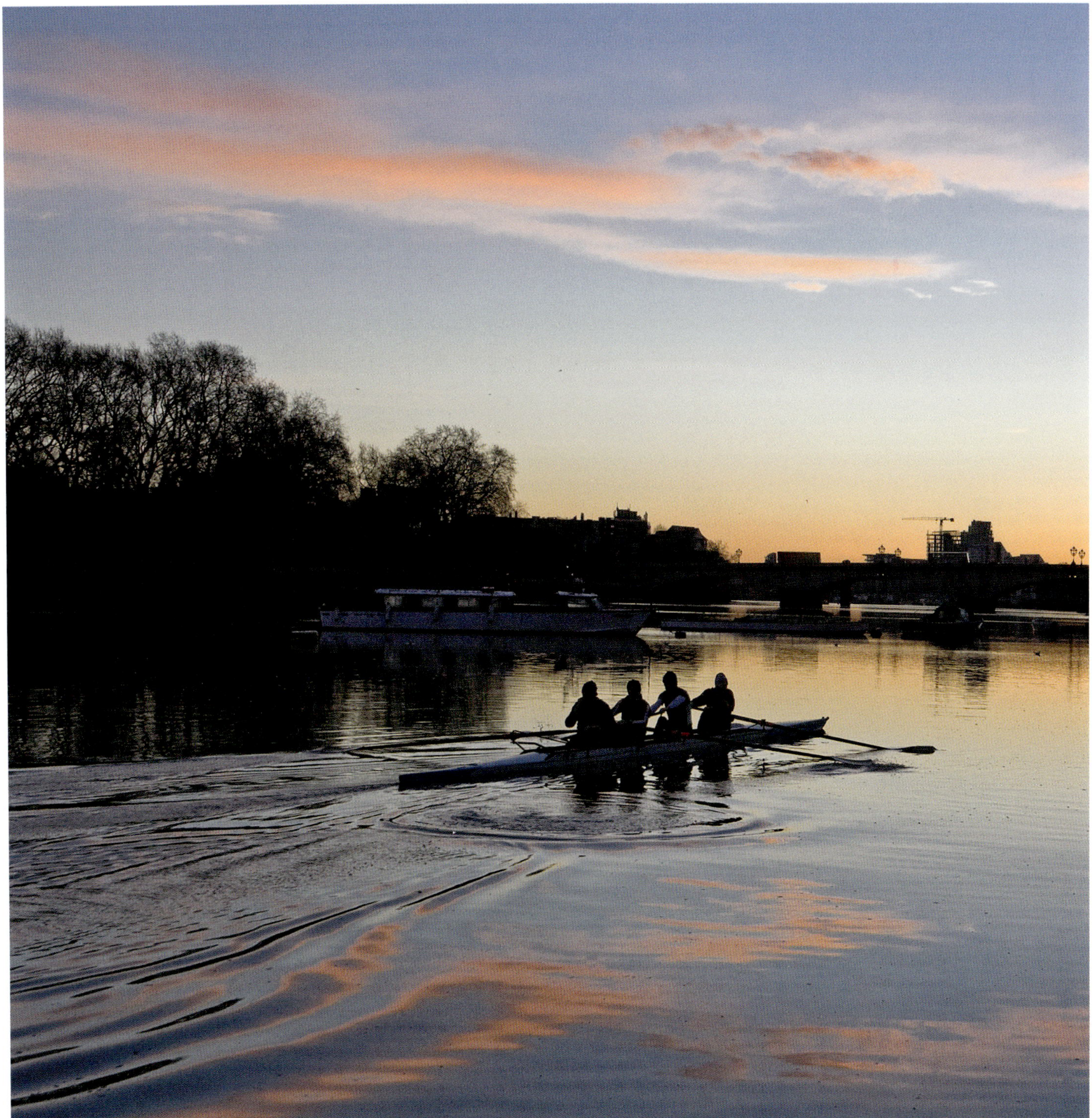

Many of the premier rowing clubs including those for London schools and universities have their headquarters overlooking the tidal reach of the Thames.

A rower uses only one oar so they row in pairs whereas scullers have two oars, one in each hand and therefore do not need another person with them in the boat.

185

For over 150 years boathouses have been a popular addition on the south bank of the river near to Putney Bridge.

In 2014 a new rowing club opened near Hammersmith Bridge, as part of the St George Fulham Reach housing development The Fulham Reach Boat Club specialises in rowing and paddle sports and is introducing new members to the joys of being on the river.

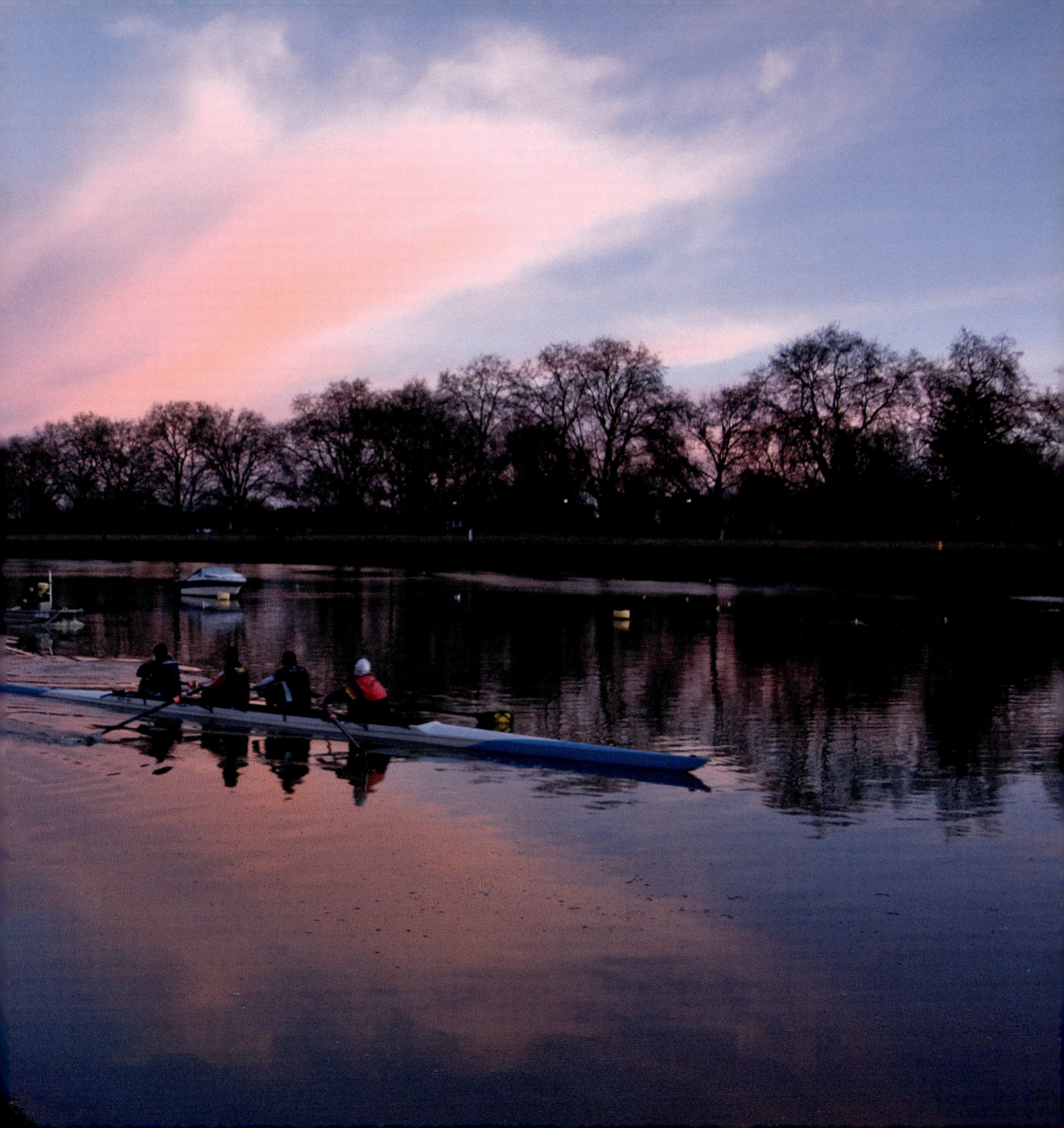

The Boat Race

The first University Boat Race in 1829 was the result of a challenge between two friends, Charles Merivale who was at Cambridge and Charles Wordsworth at Oxford and was run at Henley, only moving to its present site in 1845. Oxford went on to win the first race.

I was away throughout April 2015 so my friend and fellow photographer, James Kirkland, kindly took the photographs of this year's Boat Race for me and a grand job he did too.

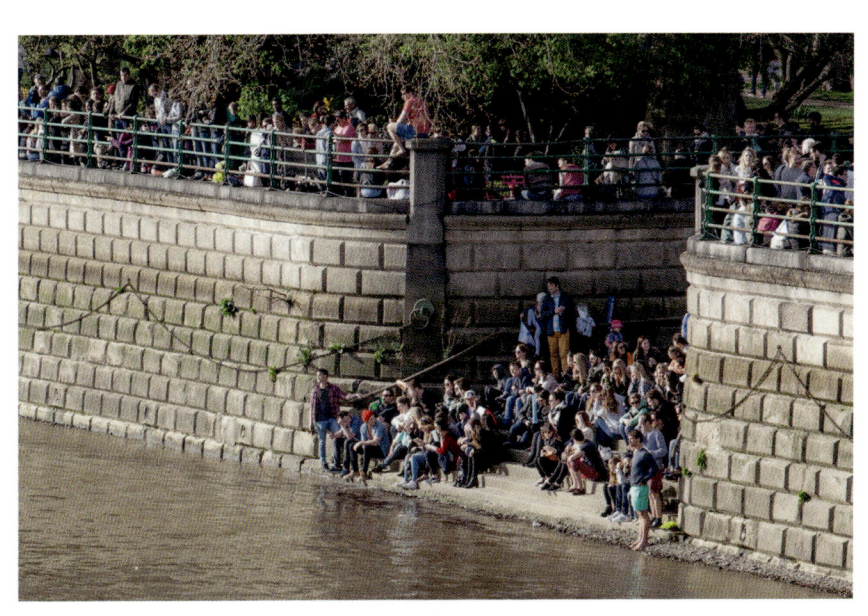

Fulham Railway and Foot Bridge

The extension of the railway line to Wimbledon in 1889 necessitated the building of a bridge across the river from Fulham to Putney. A delightful lattice girder construction, it is 418 metres long and was designed by William Jacombe, a former assistant to Isambard Kingdom Brunel.

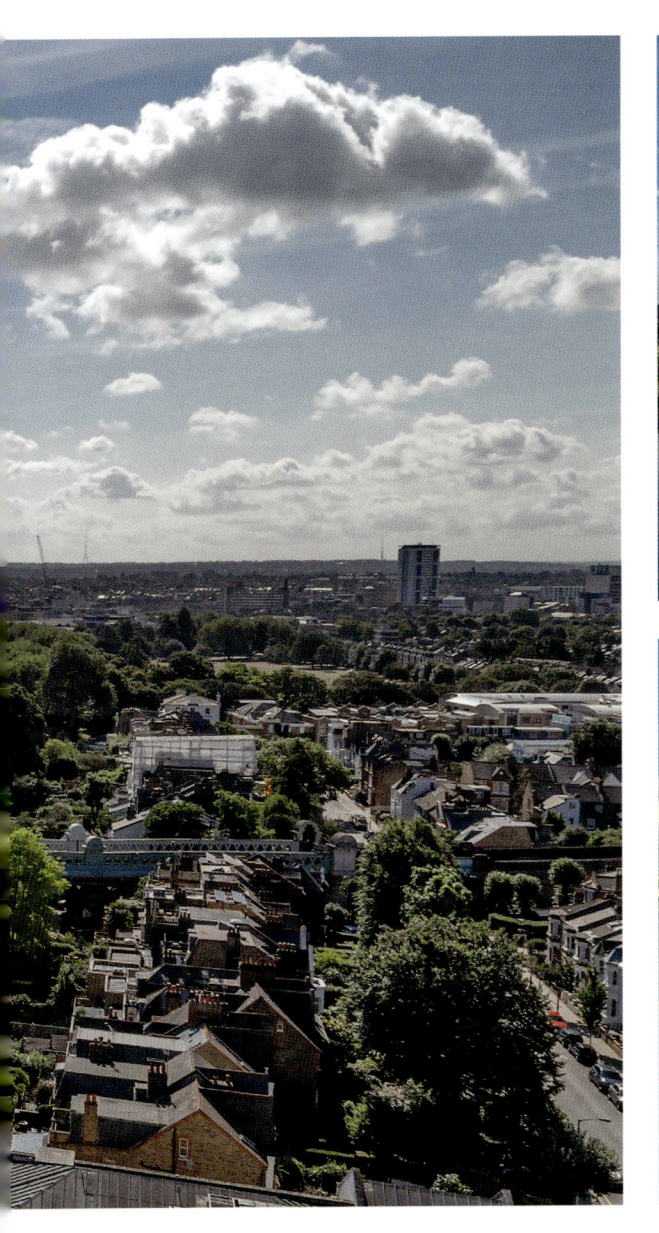

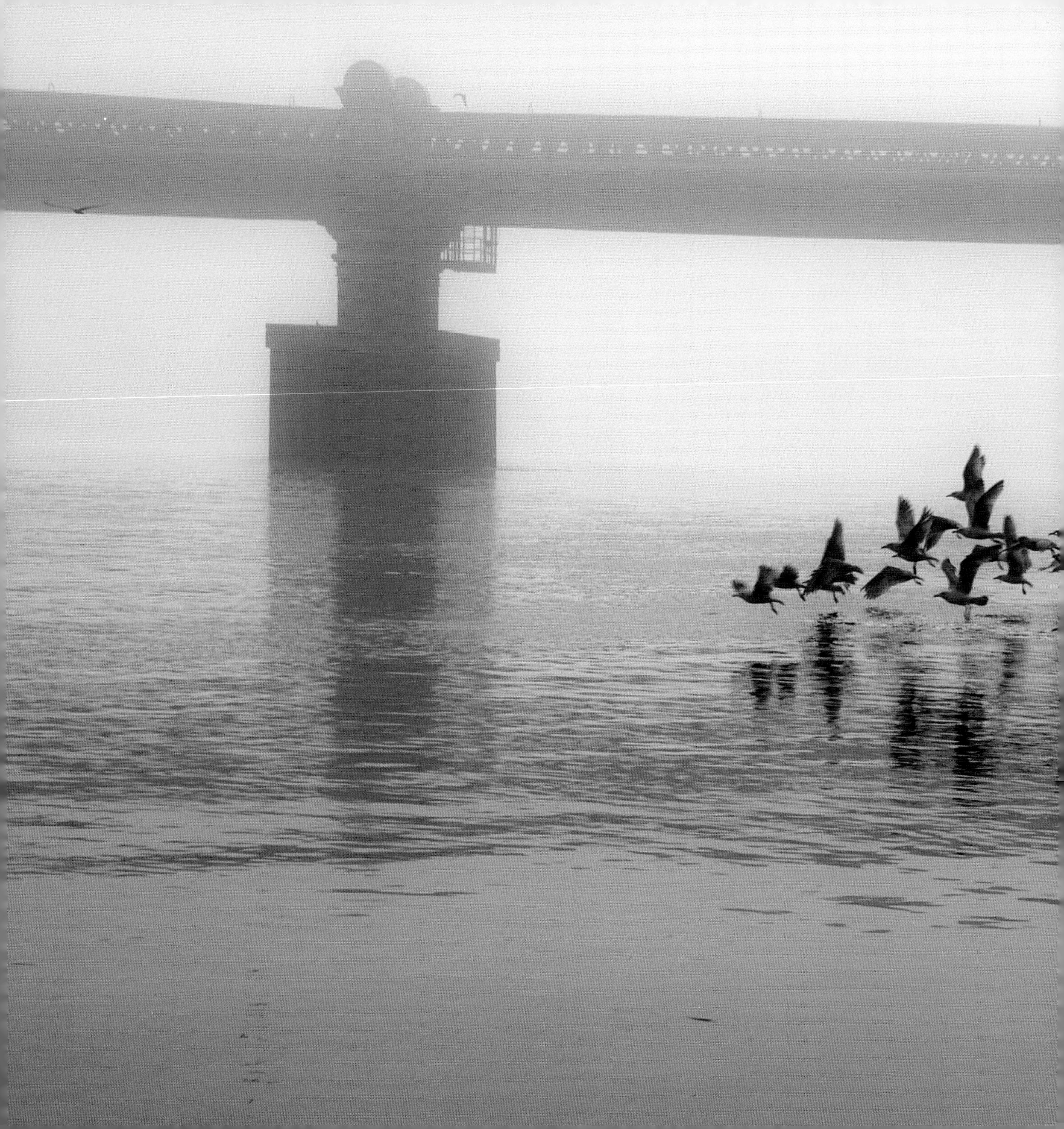

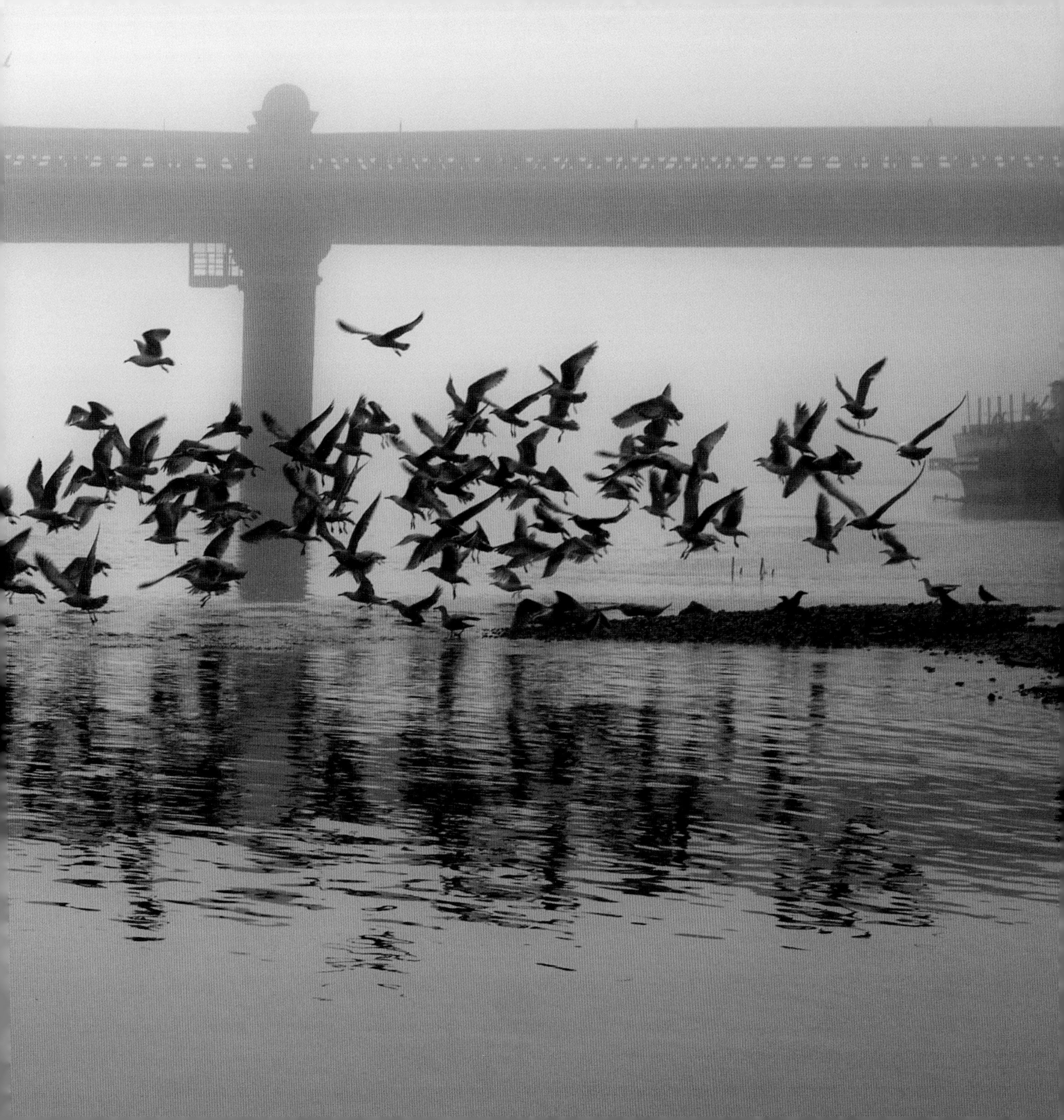

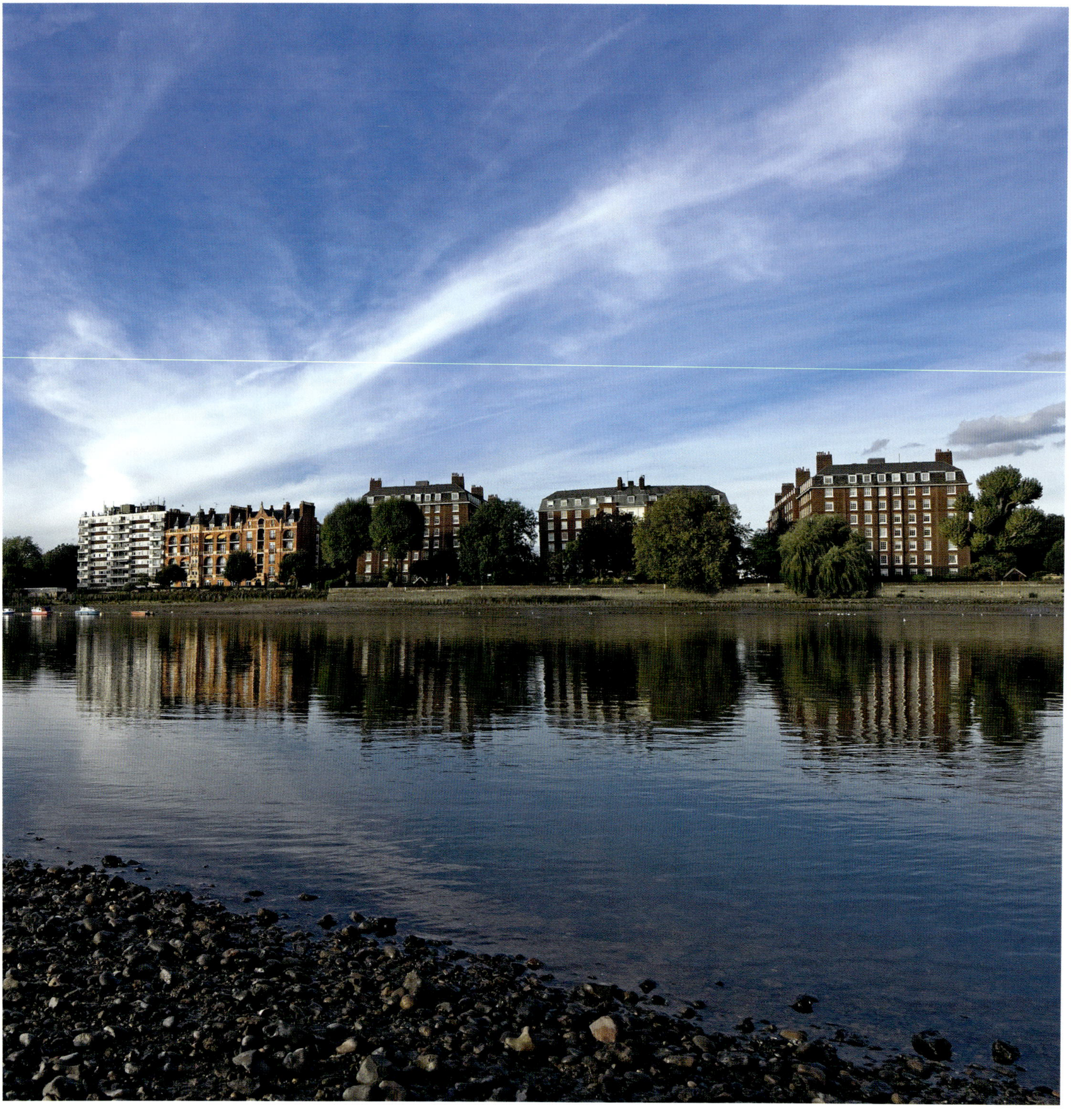

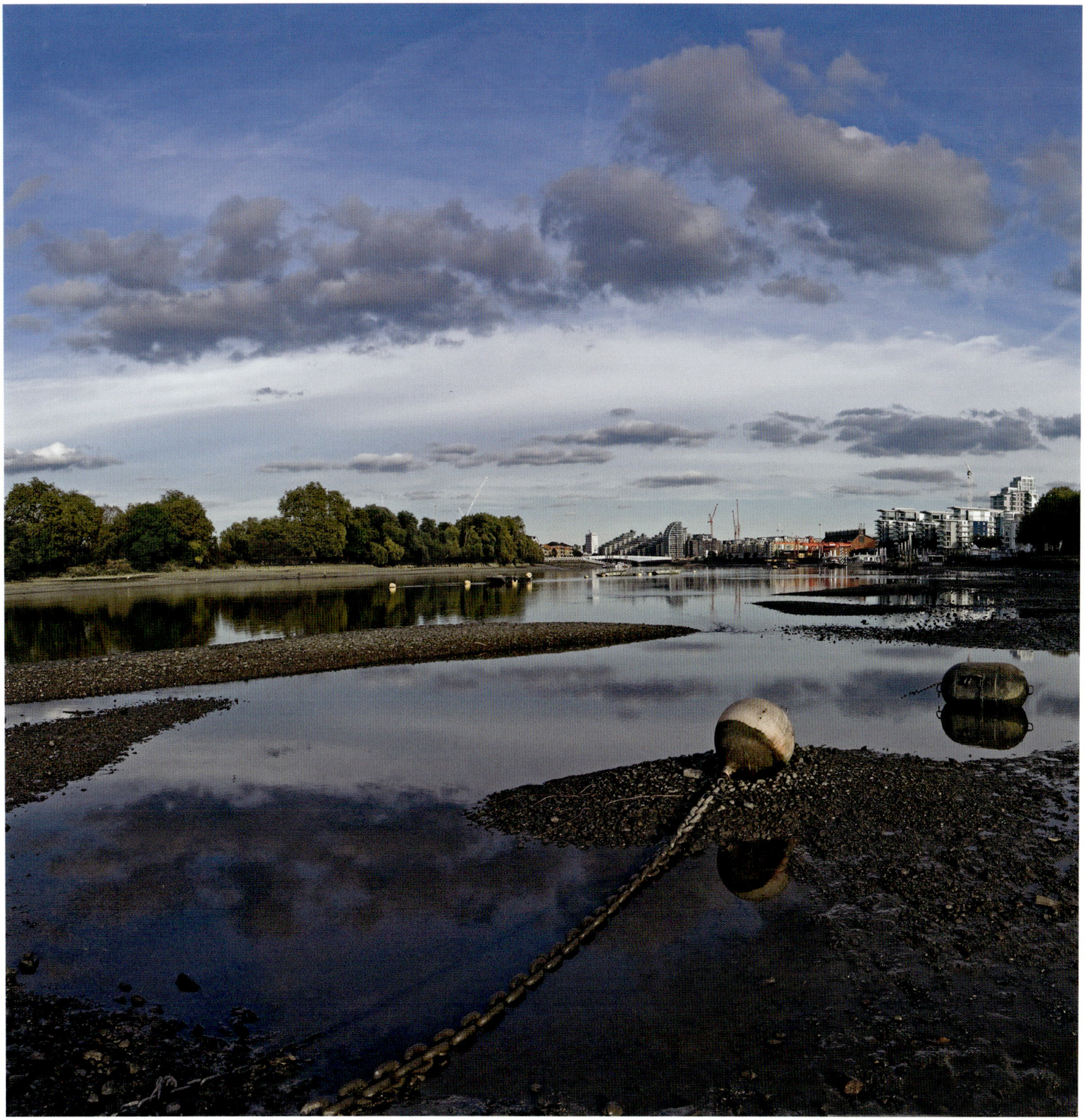

Previous pages: Riverside Mansions in Fulham from the Putney side of the river and on the right, the Thames looking east towards Wandsworth Bridge.

Above: A metal detector working the shoreline at low tide one summer's evening under Putney Bridge.

Above: The view of Putney Wharf from the shoreline beside The Hurlingham Club.

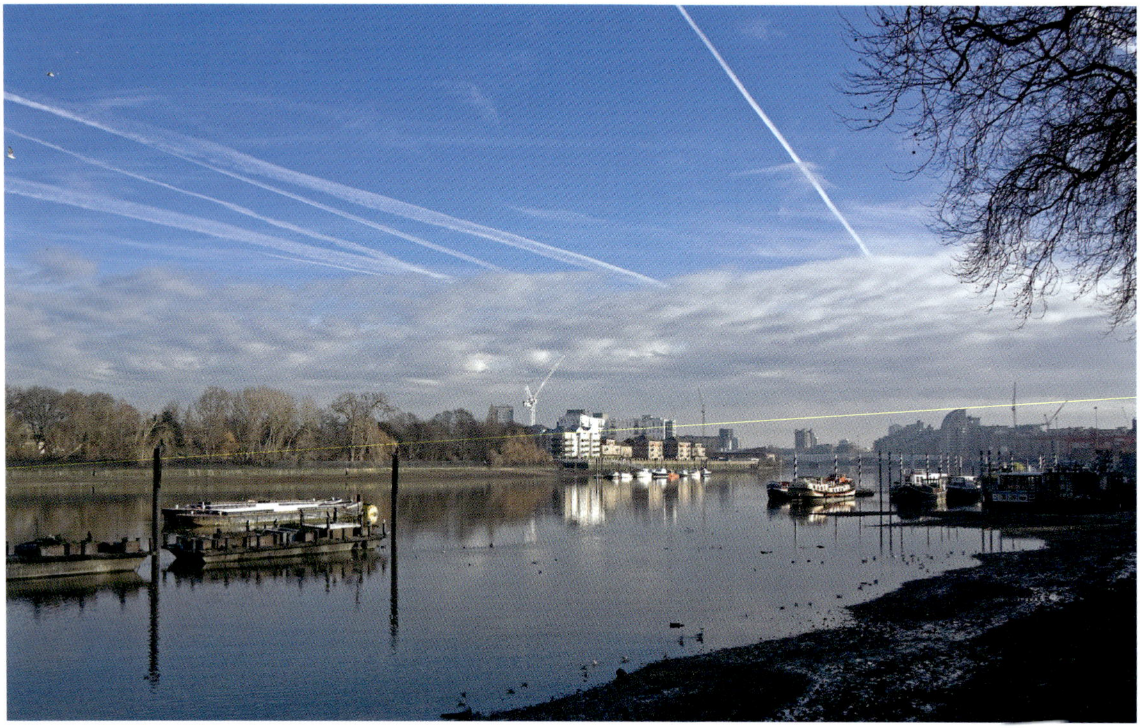

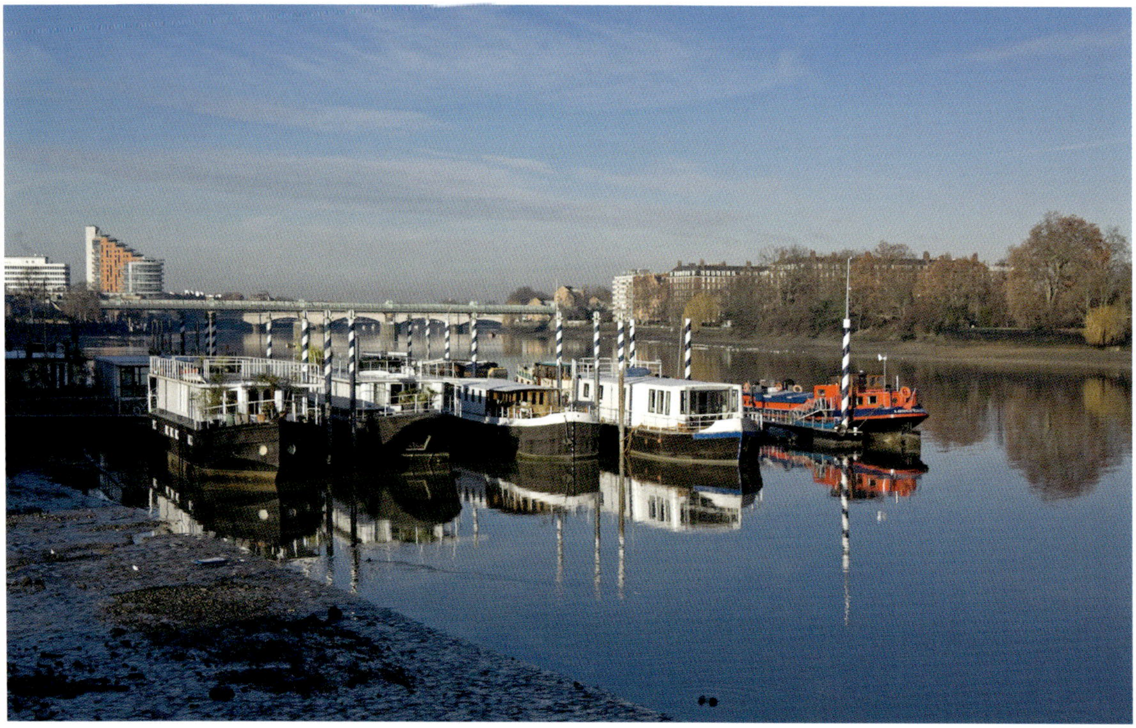

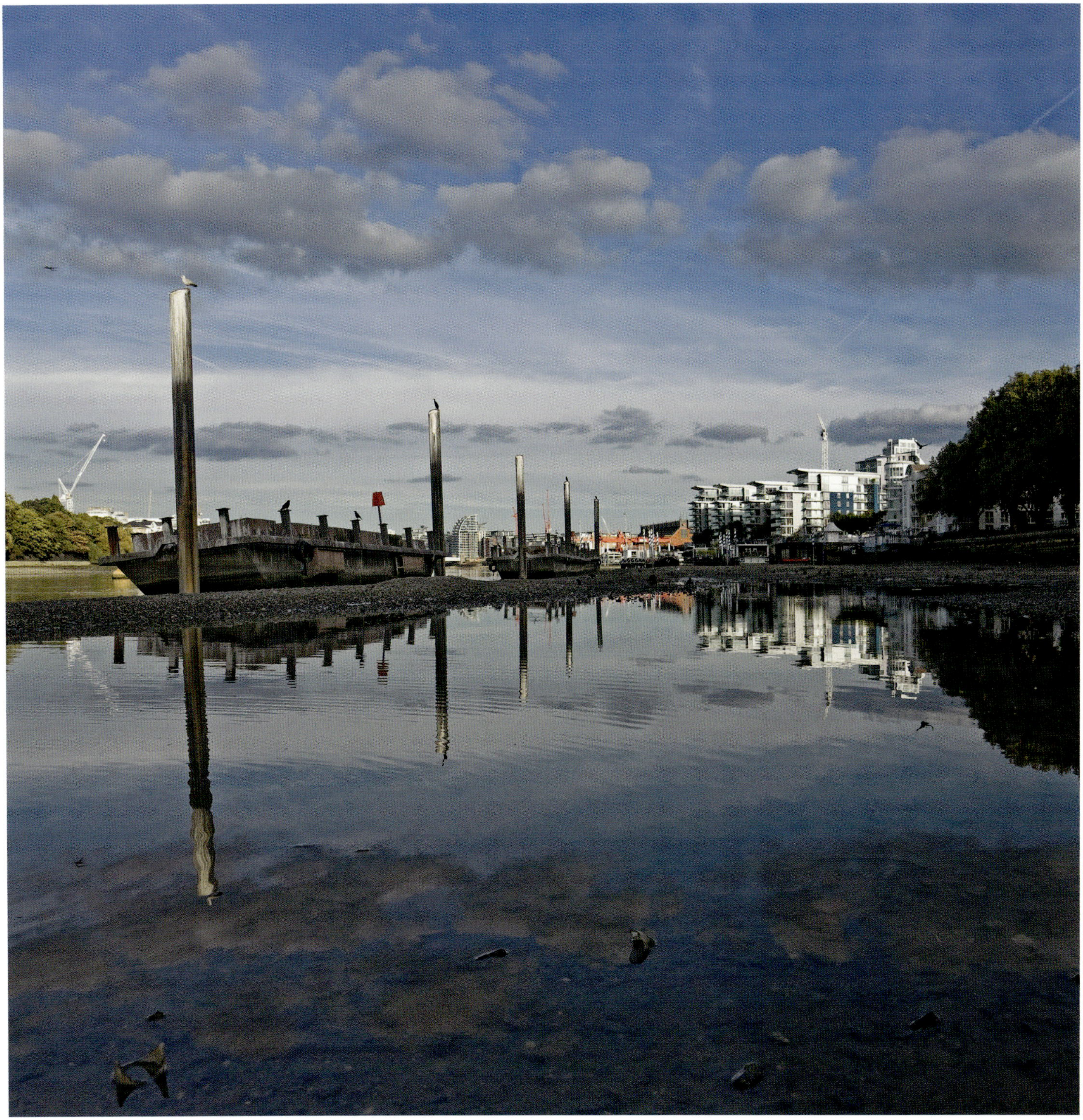

Wandsworth Bridge

Wandsworth Bridge has had some stick over the years. Local residents were disappointed with its utilitarian appearance and during the war years it was painted a dull greyish blue as a means of camouflage.

For over 50 years helicopters have flown over Fulham to and from the heliport on the Battersea bank of the river, certainly one way of beating traffic jams in the Fulham Palace Road.

For over 50 years helicopters have flown over Fulham to and from the heliport on the Battersea bank of the river, certainly one way of beating traffic jams in the Fulham Palace Road.

Thank you to Allan Fuller and all the staff at Allan Fuller Estate Agents for their kind support of my book.

ALLAN FULLER
EST. 1983

FULHAM OFFICE
963 Fulham Road
Fulham SW6 5JJ
Tel: 020 7736 2810

PUTNEY OFFICE
149 Upper Richmond Road
Putney SW15 2TX
Tel: 0208 788 8822

All rights reserved. No part of this publication may be reproduced, stored in any retrieval system or transmitted in any form or by any means, electronic, mechanical photocopying or otherwise without the prior permission of the copyright holders. Whilst every care has been taken in the production of this book, no responsibility can be accepted for any errors or omissions. The publishers have taken all reasonable care in compiling this work but cannot accept responsibility for the information derived from third parties, which has been reproduced in good faith.

First Edition – © Unity Print and Publishing Limited 2015

Designed by Ball Design & Branding
www.balldesignconsultancy.com

Printed by Page Brothers of Norwich, Norfolk.
www.pagebros.co.uk

Colour Management by Paul Sherfield of The Missing Horse Consultancy.
www.missinghorsecons.co.uk

Publishing Assistant: Alexis Wilson

Published by Unity Print and Publishing Limited,
18 Dungarvan Avenue,
London SW15 5QU.
Tel: +44 (0)20 8487 2199
aw@unity-publishing.co.uk
www.unity-publishing.co.uk

Thank you to Frank Harrington and all the staff at Atlantic Plumbing & Heating for their kind support of my book.

ATLANTIC

6–8 Peterborough Mews, Fulham, London SW6 3BL
Tel: 020 7736 0303   Email: service@atlanticplumbing.co.uk

Budgens
Discover local foods & big brands

227-233 Munster Road
SW6 6BT

57-69 Parsons Green Lane
SW6 4JA

Follow Andrew on Twitter:
@andrewpics

204

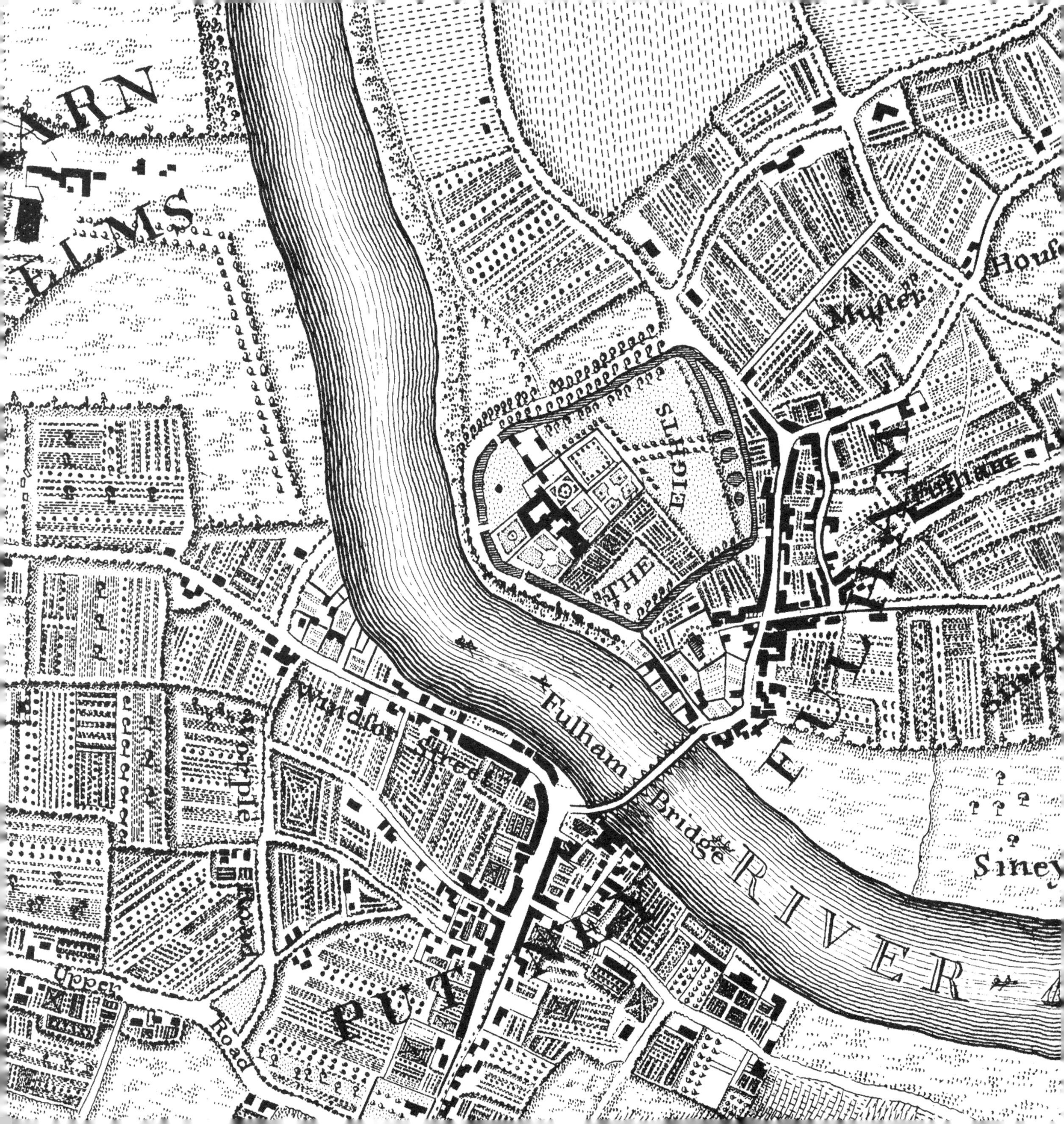
ARN
ELMS
THE EIGHTS
Fulham
Bridge
RIVER
Upper
Road
Siney